C-113 CAREER EXAMINATION SERIES

This is your PASSBOOK for...

School Transportation Supervisor

Test Preparation Study Guide Questions & Answers

NLC®
NATIONAL LEARNING CORPORATION®

National Learning Corporation

212 Michael Drive, Syosset, NY 11791
(516) 921-8888 • www.passbooks.com
E-mail: info@passbooks.com

PUBLISHED IN THE UNITED STATES OF AMERICA

PASSBOOK® SERIES

THE *PASSBOOK® SERIES* has been created to prepare applicants and candidates for the ultimate academic battlefield – the examination room.

At some time in our lives, each and every one of us may be required to take an examination – for validation, matriculation, admission, qualification, registration, certification, or licensure.

Based on the assumption that every applicant or candidate has met the basic formal educational standards, has taken the required number of courses, and read the necessary texts, the *PASSBOOK® SERIES* furnishes the one special preparation which may assure passing with confidence, instead of failing with insecurity. Examination questions – together with answers – are furnished as the basic vehicle for study so that the mysteries of the examination and its compounding difficulties may be eliminated or diminished by a sure method.

This book is meant to help you pass your examination provided that you qualify and are serious in your objective.

The entire field is reviewed through the huge store of content information which is succinctly presented through a provocative and challenging approach – the question-and-answer method.

A climate of success is established by furnishing the correct answers at the end of each test.

You soon learn to recognize types of questions, forms of questions, and patterns of questioning. You may even begin to anticipate expected outcomes.

You perceive that many questions are repeated or adapted so that you can gain acute insights, which may enable you to score many sure points.

You learn how to confront new questions, or types of questions, and to attack them confidently and work out the correct answers.

You note objectives and emphases, and recognize pitfalls and dangers, so that you may make positive educational adjustments.

Moreover, you are kept fully informed in relation to new concepts, methods, practices, and directions in the field.

You discover that you are actually taking the examination all the time: you are preparing for the examination by "taking" an examination, not by reading extraneous and/or supererogatory textbooks.

In short, this PASSBOOK®, used directedly, should be an important factor in helping you to pass your test.

SCHOOL TRANSPORTATION SUPERVISOR

DUTIES
Performs highly responsible administrative duties in directing the school transportation program for a large school district. Plans, assigns, and directs the work of subordinate employees engaged in the operation and maintenance of school transportation equipment. Establishes bus routes and time schedules for each school. Supervises the maintenance, repair, and inspection of all vehicles in the district. Prepares personnel, budget, maintenance, and state inspection reports and records. Prepares requisitions and specifications for all transportation equipment, parts, and supplies. Advises the board of education on present and future transportation needs and costs. Performs related work as required.

SCOPE OF THE EXAMINATION
The multiple-choice test cover knowledge's, skills, and/or abilities in the following are as:

1. Scheduling work and equipment;
2. Supervision;
3. Record keeping;
4. Operation of motor vehicles;
5. School transportation management; and
6. Maintenance and repair of motor vehicles, including tools and test equipment.

HOW TO TAKE A TEST

I. YOU MUST PASS AN EXAMINATION

A. WHAT EVERY CANDIDATE SHOULD KNOW

Examination applicants often ask us for help in preparing for the written test. What can I study in advance? What kinds of questions will be asked? How will the test be given? How will the papers be graded?

As an applicant for a civil service examination, you may be wondering about some of these things. Our purpose here is to suggest effective methods of advance study and to describe civil service examinations.

Your chances for success on this examination can be increased if you know how to prepare. Those "pre-examination jitters" can be reduced if you know what to expect. You can even experience an adventure in good citizenship if you know why civil service exams are given.

B. WHY ARE CIVIL SERVICE EXAMINATIONS GIVEN?

Civil service examinations are important to you in two ways. As a citizen, you want public jobs filled by employees who know how to do their work. As a job seeker, you want a fair chance to compete for that job on an equal footing with other candidates. The best-known means of accomplishing this two-fold goal is the competitive examination.

Exams are widely publicized throughout the nation. They may be administered for jobs in federal, state, city, municipal, town or village governments or agencies.

Any citizen may apply, with some limitations, such as the age or residence of applicants. Your experience and education may be reviewed to see whether you meet the requirements for the particular examination. When these requirements exist, they are reasonable and applied consistently to all applicants. Thus, a competitive examination may cause you some uneasiness now, but it is your privilege and safeguard.

C. HOW ARE CIVIL SERVICE EXAMS DEVELOPED?

Examinations are carefully written by trained technicians who are specialists in the field known as "psychological measurement," in consultation with recognized authorities in the field of work that the test will cover. These experts recommend the subject matter areas or skills to be tested; only those knowledges or skills important to your success on the job are included. The most reliable books and source materials available are used as references. Together, the experts and technicians judge the difficulty level of the questions.

Test technicians know how to phrase questions so that the problem is clearly stated. Their ethics do not permit "trick" or "catch" questions. Questions may have been tried out on sample groups, or subjected to statistical analysis, to determine their usefulness.

Written tests are often used in combination with performance tests, ratings of training and experience, and oral interviews. All of these measures combine to form the best-known means of finding the right person for the right job.

II. HOW TO PASS THE WRITTEN TEST

A. NATURE OF THE EXAMINATION

To prepare intelligently for civil service examinations, you should know how they differ from school examinations you have taken. In school you were assigned certain definite pages to read or subjects to cover. The examination questions were quite detailed and usually emphasized memory. Civil service exams, on the other hand, try to discover your present ability to perform the duties of a position, plus your potentiality to learn these duties. In other words, a civil service exam attempts to predict how successful you will be. Questions cover such a broad area that they cannot be as minute and detailed as school exam questions.

In the public service similar kinds of work, or positions, are grouped together in one "class." This process is known as *position-classification*. All the positions in a class are paid according to the salary range for that class. One class title covers all of these positions, and they are all tested by the same examination.

B. FOUR BASIC STEPS

1) Study the announcement

How, then, can you know what subjects to study? Our best answer is: "Learn as much as possible about the class of positions for which you've applied." The exam will test the knowledge, skills and abilities needed to do the work.

Your most valuable source of information about the position you want is the official exam announcement. This announcement lists the training and experience qualifications. Check these standards and apply only if you come reasonably close to meeting them.

The brief description of the position in the examination announcement offers some clues to the subjects which will be tested. Think about the job itself. Review the duties in your mind. Can you perform them, or are there some in which you are rusty? Fill in the blank spots in your preparation.

Many jurisdictions preview the written test in the exam announcement by including a section called "Knowledge and Abilities Required," "Scope of the Examination," or some similar heading. Here you will find out specifically what fields will be tested.

2) Review your own background

Once you learn in general what the position is all about, and what you need to know to do the work, ask yourself which subjects you already know fairly well and which need improvement. You may wonder whether to concentrate on improving your strong areas or on building some background in your fields of weakness. When the announcement has specified "some knowledge" or "considerable knowledge," or has used adjectives like "beginning principles of..." or "advanced ... methods," you can get a clue as to the number and difficulty of questions to be asked in any given field. More questions, and hence broader coverage, would be included for those subjects which are more important in the work. Now weigh your strengths and weaknesses against the job requirements and prepare accordingly.

3) Determine the level of the position

Another way to tell how intensively you should prepare is to understand the level of the job for which you are applying. Is it the entering level? In other words, is this the position in which beginners in a field of work are hired? Or is it an intermediate or advanced level? Sometimes this is indicated by such words as "Junior" or "Senior" in the class title. Other jurisdictions use Roman numerals to designate the level – Clerk I, Clerk II, for example. The word "Supervisor" sometimes appears in the title. If the level is not indicated by the title, check the description of duties. Will you be working under very close supervision, or will you have responsibility for independent decisions in this work?

4) Choose appropriate study materials

Now that you know the subjects to be examined and the relative amount of each subject to be covered, you can choose suitable study materials. For beginning level jobs, or even advanced ones, if you have a pronounced weakness in some aspect of your training, read a modern, standard textbook in that field. Be sure it is up to date and has general coverage. Such books are normally available at your library, and the librarian will be glad to help you locate one. For entry-level positions, questions of appropriate difficulty are chosen – neither highly advanced questions, nor those too simple. Such questions require careful thought but not advanced training.

If the position for which you are applying is technical or advanced, you will read more advanced, specialized material. If you are already familiar with the basic principles of your field, elementary textbooks would waste your time. Concentrate on advanced textbooks and technical periodicals. Think through the concepts and review difficult problems in your field.

These are all general sources. You can get more ideas on your own initiative, following these leads. For example, training manuals and publications of the government agency which employs workers in your field can be useful, particularly for technical and professional positions. A letter or visit to the government department involved may result in more specific study suggestions, and certainly will provide you with a more definite idea of the exact nature of the position you are seeking.

III. KINDS OF TESTS

Tests are used for purposes other than measuring knowledge and ability to perform specified duties. For some positions, it is equally important to test ability to make adjustments to new situations or to profit from training. In others, basic mental abilities not dependent on information are essential. Questions which test these things may not appear as pertinent to the duties of the position as those which test for knowledge and information. Yet they are often highly important parts of a fair examination. For very general questions, it is almost impossible to help you direct your study efforts. What we can do is to point out some of the more common of these general abilities needed in public service positions and describe some typical questions.

1) General information

Broad, general information has been found useful for predicting job success in some kinds of work. This is tested in a variety of ways, from vocabulary lists to questions about current events. Basic background in some field of work, such as sociology or economics, may be sampled in a group of questions. Often these are principles which have become familiar to most persons through exposure rather than through formal training. It is difficult to advise you how to study for these questions; being alert to the world around you is our best suggestion.

2) Verbal ability

An example of an ability needed in many positions is verbal or language ability. Verbal ability is, in brief, the ability to use and understand words. Vocabulary and grammar tests are typical measures of this ability. Reading comprehension or paragraph interpretation questions are common in many kinds of civil service tests. You are given a paragraph of written material and asked to find its central meaning.

3) Numerical ability

Number skills can be tested by the familiar arithmetic problem, by checking paired lists of numbers to see which are alike and which are different, or by interpreting charts and graphs. In the latter test, a graph may be printed in the test booklet which you are asked to use as the basis for answering questions.

4) Observation

A popular test for law-enforcement positions is the observation test. A picture is shown to you for several minutes, then taken away. Questions about the picture test your ability to observe both details and larger elements.

5) Following directions

In many positions in the public service, the employee must be able to carry out written instructions dependably and accurately. You may be given a chart with several columns, each column listing a variety of information. The questions require you to carry out directions involving the information given in the chart.

6) Skills and aptitudes

Performance tests effectively measure some manual skills and aptitudes. When the skill is one in which you are trained, such as typing or shorthand, you can practice. These tests are often very much like those given in business school or high school courses. For many of the other skills and aptitudes, however, no short-time preparation can be made. Skills and abilities natural to you or that you have developed throughout your lifetime are being tested.

Many of the general questions just described provide all the data needed to answer the questions and ask you to use your reasoning ability to find the answers. Your best preparation for these tests, as well as for tests of facts and ideas, is to be at your physical and mental best. You, no doubt, have your own methods of getting into an exam-taking mood and keeping "in shape." The next section lists some ideas on this subject.

IV. KINDS OF QUESTIONS

Only rarely is the "essay" question, which you answer in narrative form, used in civil service tests. Civil service tests are usually of the short-answer type. Full instructions for answering these questions will be given to you at the examination. But in case this is your first experience with short-answer questions and separate answer sheets, here is what you need to know:

1) Multiple-choice Questions

Most popular of the short-answer questions is the "multiple choice" or "best answer" question. It can be used, for example, to test for factual knowledge, ability to solve problems or judgment in meeting situations found at work.

A multiple-choice question is normally one of three types—

- It can begin with an incomplete statement followed by several possible endings. You are to find the one ending which *best* completes the statement, although some of the others may not be entirely wrong.
- It can also be a complete statement in the form of a question which is answered by choosing one of the statements listed.

- It can be in the form of a problem – again you select the best answer.

Here is an example of a multiple-choice question with a discussion which should give you some clues as to the method for choosing the right answer:

When an employee has a complaint about his assignment, the action which will *best* help him overcome his difficulty is to

A. discuss his difficulty with his coworkers
B. take the problem to the head of the organization
C. take the problem to the person who gave him the assignment
D. say nothing to anyone about his complaint

In answering this question, you should study each of the choices to find which is best. Consider choice "A" – Certainly an employee may discuss his complaint with fellow employees, but no change or improvement can result, and the complaint remains unresolved. Choice "B" is a poor choice since the head of the organization probably does not know what assignment you have been given, and taking your problem to him is known as "going over the head" of the supervisor. The supervisor, or person who made the assignment, is the person who can clarify it or correct any injustice. Choice "C" is, therefore, correct. To say nothing, as in choice "D," is unwise. Supervisors have and interest in knowing the problems employees are facing, and the employee is seeking a solution to his problem.

2) True/False Questions

The "true/false" or "right/wrong" form of question is sometimes used. Here a complete statement is given. Your job is to decide whether the statement is right or wrong.

SAMPLE: A roaming cell-phone call to a nearby city costs less than a non-roaming call to a distant city.

This statement is wrong, or false, since roaming calls are more expensive.

This is not a complete list of all possible question forms, although most of the others are variations of these common types. You will always get complete directions for answering questions. Be sure you understand *how* to mark your answers – ask questions until you do.

V. RECORDING YOUR ANSWERS

Computer terminals are used more and more today for many different kinds of exams.

For an examination with very few applicants, you may be told to record your answers in the test booklet itself. Separate answer sheets are much more common. If this separate answer sheet is to be scored by machine – and this is often the case – it is highly important that you mark your answers correctly in order to get credit.

An electronic scoring machine is often used in civil service offices because of the speed with which papers can be scored. Machine-scored answer sheets must be marked with a pencil, which will be given to you. This pencil has a high graphite content which responds to the electronic scoring machine. As a matter of fact, stray dots may register as answers, so do not let your pencil rest on the answer sheet while you are pondering the correct answer. Also, if your pencil lead breaks or is otherwise defective, ask for another.

Since the answer sheet will be dropped in a slot in the scoring machine, be careful not to bend the corners or get the paper crumpled.

The answer sheet normally has five vertical columns of numbers, with 30 numbers to a column. These numbers correspond to the question numbers in your test booklet. After each number, going across the page are four or five pairs of dotted lines. These short dotted lines have small letters or numbers above them. The first two pairs may also have a "T" or "F" above the letters. This indicates that the first two pairs only are to be used if the questions are of the true-false type. If the questions are multiple choice, disregard the "T" and "F" and pay attention only to the small letters or numbers.

Answer your questions in the manner of the sample that follows:

32. The largest city in the United States is
    A. Washington, D.C.
    B. New York City
    C. Chicago
    D. Detroit
    E. San Francisco

1) Choose the answer you think is best. (New York City is the largest, so "B" is correct.)
2) Find the row of dotted lines numbered the same as the question you are answering. (Find row number 32)
3) Find the pair of dotted lines corresponding to the answer. (Find the pair of lines under the mark "B.")
4) Make a solid black mark between the dotted lines.

VI. BEFORE THE TEST

Common sense will help you find procedures to follow to get ready for an examination. Too many of us, however, overlook these sensible measures. Indeed, nervousness and fatigue have been found to be the most serious reasons why applicants fail to do their best on civil service tests. Here is a list of reminders:

- Begin your preparation early – Don't wait until the last minute to go scurrying around for books and materials or to find out what the position is all about.
- Prepare continuously – An hour a night for a week is better than an all-night cram session. This has been definitely established. What is more, a night a week for a month will return better dividends than crowding your study into a shorter period of time.
- Locate the place of the exam – You have been sent a notice telling you when and where to report for the examination. If the location is in a different town or otherwise unfamiliar to you, it would be well to inquire the best route and learn something about the building.
- Relax the night before the test – Allow your mind to rest. Do not study at all that night. Plan some mild recreation or diversion; then go to bed early and get a good night's sleep.
- Get up early enough to make a leisurely trip to the place for the test – This way unforeseen events, traffic snarls, unfamiliar buildings, etc. will not upset you.
- Dress comfortably – A written test is not a fashion show. You will be known by number and not by name, so wear something comfortable.

- Leave excess paraphernalia at home – Shopping bags and odd bundles will get in your way. You need bring only the items mentioned in the official notice you received; usually everything you need is provided. Do not bring reference books to the exam. They will only confuse those last minutes and be taken away from you when in the test room.
- Arrive somewhat ahead of time – If because of transportation schedules you must get there very early, bring a newspaper or magazine to take your mind off yourself while waiting.
- Locate the examination room – When you have found the proper room, you will be directed to the seat or part of the room where you will sit. Sometimes you are given a sheet of instructions to read while you are waiting. Do not fill out any forms until you are told to do so; just read them and be prepared.
- Relax and prepare to listen to the instructions
- If you have any physical problem that may keep you from doing your best, be sure to tell the test administrator. If you are sick or in poor health, you really cannot do your best on the exam. You can come back and take the test some other time.

VII. AT THE TEST

The day of the test is here and you have the test booklet in your hand. The temptation to get going is very strong. Caution! There is more to success than knowing the right answers. You must know how to identify your papers and understand variations in the type of short-answer question used in this particular examination. Follow these suggestions for maximum results from your efforts:

1) Cooperate with the monitor

The test administrator has a duty to create a situation in which you can be as much at ease as possible. He will give instructions, tell you when to begin, check to see that you are marking your answer sheet correctly, and so on. He is not there to guard you, although he will see that your competitors do not take unfair advantage. He wants to help you do your best.

2) Listen to all instructions

Don't jump the gun! Wait until you understand all directions. In most civil service tests you get more time than you need to answer the questions. So don't be in a hurry. Read each word of instructions until you clearly understand the meaning. Study the examples, listen to all announcements and follow directions. Ask questions if you do not understand what to do.

3) Identify your papers

Civil service exams are usually identified by number only. You will be assigned a number; you must not put your name on your test papers. Be sure to copy your number correctly. Since more than one exam may be given, copy your exact examination title.

4) Plan your time

Unless you are told that a test is a "speed" or "rate of work" test, speed itself is usually not important. Time enough to answer all the questions will be provided, but this does not mean that you have all day. An overall time limit has been set. Divide the total time (in minutes) by the number of questions to determine the approximate time you have for each question.

5) Do not linger over difficult questions

If you come across a difficult question, mark it with a paper clip (useful to have along) and come back to it when you have been through the booklet. One caution if you do this – be sure to skip a number on your answer sheet as well. Check often to be sure that you have not lost your place and that you are marking in the row numbered the same as the question you are answering.

6) Read the questions

Be sure you know what the question asks! Many capable people are unsuccessful because they failed to *read* the questions correctly.

7) Answer all questions

Unless you have been instructed that a penalty will be deducted for incorrect answers, it is better to guess than to omit a question.

8) Speed tests

It is often better NOT to guess on speed tests. It has been found that on timed tests people are tempted to spend the last few seconds before time is called in marking answers at random – without even reading them – in the hope of picking up a few extra points. To discourage this practice, the instructions may warn you that your score will be "corrected" for guessing. That is, a penalty will be applied. The incorrect answers will be deducted from the correct ones, or some other penalty formula will be used.

9) Review your answers

If you finish before time is called, go back to the questions you guessed or omitted to give them further thought. Review other answers if you have time.

10) Return your test materials

If you are ready to leave before others have finished or time is called, take ALL your materials to the monitor and leave quietly. Never take any test material with you. The monitor can discover whose papers are not complete, and taking a test booklet may be grounds for disqualification.

VIII. EXAMINATION TECHNIQUES

1) Read the general instructions carefully. These are usually printed on the first page of the exam booklet. As a rule, these instructions refer to the timing of the examination; the fact that you should not start work until the signal and must stop work at a signal, etc. If there are any *special* instructions, such as a choice of questions to be answered, make sure that you note this instruction carefully.

2) When you are ready to start work on the examination, that is as soon as the signal has been given, read the instructions to each question booklet, underline any key words or phrases, such as *least*, *best*, *outline*, *describe* and the like. In this way you will tend to answer as requested rather than discover on reviewing your paper that you *listed without describing*, that you selected the *worst* choice rather than the *best* choice, etc.

3) If the examination is of the objective or multiple-choice type – that is, each question will also give a series of possible answers: A, B, C or D, and you are called upon to select the best answer and write the letter next to that answer on your answer paper – it is advisable to start answering each question in turn. There may be anywhere from 50 to 100 such questions in the three or four hours allotted and you can see how much time would be taken if you read through all the questions before beginning to answer any. Furthermore, if you come across a question or group of questions which you know would be difficult to answer, it would undoubtedly affect your handling of all the other questions.

4) If the examination is of the essay type and contains but a few questions, it is a moot point as to whether you should read all the questions before starting to answer any one. Of course, if you are given a choice – say five out of seven and the like – then it is essential to read all the questions so you can eliminate the two that are most difficult. If, however, you are asked to answer all the questions, there may be danger in trying to answer the easiest one first because you may find that you will spend too much time on it. The best technique is to answer the first question, then proceed to the second, etc.

5) Time your answers. Before the exam begins, write down the time it started, then add the time allowed for the examination and write down the time it must be completed, then divide the time available somewhat as follows:
   - If 3-1/2 hours are allowed, that would be 210 minutes. If you have 80 objective-type questions, that would be an average of 2-1/2 minutes per question. Allow yourself no more than 2 minutes per question, or a total of 160 minutes, which will permit about 50 minutes to review.
   - If for the time allotment of 210 minutes there are 7 essay questions to answer, that would average about 30 minutes a question. Give yourself only 25 minutes per question so that you have about 35 minutes to review.

6) The most important instruction is to *read each question* and make sure you know what is wanted. The second most important instruction is to *time yourself properly* so that you answer every question. The third most important instruction is to *answer every question*. Guess if you have to but include something for each question. Remember that you will receive no credit for a blank and will probably receive some credit if you write something in answer to an essay question. If you guess a letter – say "B" for a multiple-choice question – you may have guessed right. If you leave a blank as an answer to a multiple-choice question, the examiners may respect your feelings but it will not add a point to your score. Some exams may penalize you for wrong answers, so in such cases *only*, you may not want to guess unless you have some basis for your answer.

7) Suggestions
   a. Objective-type questions
      1. Examine the question booklet for proper sequence of pages and questions
      2. Read all instructions carefully
      3. Skip any question which seems too difficult; return to it after all other questions have been answered
      4. Apportion your time properly; do not spend too much time on any single question or group of questions

5. Note and underline key words – *all, most, fewest, least, best, worst, same, opposite*, etc.
6. Pay particular attention to negatives
7. Note unusual option, e.g., unduly long, short, complex, different or similar in content to the body of the question
8. Observe the use of "hedging" words – *probably, may, most likely*, etc.
9. Make sure that your answer is put next to the same number as the question
10. Do not second-guess unless you have good reason to believe the second answer is definitely more correct
11. Cross out original answer if you decide another answer is more accurate; do not erase until you are ready to hand your paper in
12. Answer all questions; guess unless instructed otherwise
13. Leave time for review

b. Essay questions
1. Read each question carefully
2. Determine exactly what is wanted. Underline key words or phrases.
3. Decide on outline or paragraph answer
4. Include many different points and elements unless asked to develop any one or two points or elements
5. Show impartiality by giving pros and cons unless directed to select one side only
6. Make and write down any assumptions you find necessary to answer the questions
7. Watch your English, grammar, punctuation and choice of words
8. Time your answers; don't crowd material

8) Answering the essay question

Most essay questions can be answered by framing the specific response around several key words or ideas. Here are a few such key words or ideas:

M's: manpower, materials, methods, money, management
P's: purpose, program, policy, plan, procedure, practice, problems, pitfalls, personnel, public relations

a. Six basic steps in handling problems:
1. Preliminary plan and background development
2. Collect information, data and facts
3. Analyze and interpret information, data and facts
4. Analyze and develop solutions as well as make recommendations
5. Prepare report and sell recommendations
6. Install recommendations and follow up effectiveness

b. Pitfalls to avoid
1. *Taking things for granted* – A statement of the situation does not necessarily imply that each of the elements is necessarily true; for example, a complaint may be invalid and biased so that all that can be taken for granted is that a complaint has been registered

2. *Considering only one side of a situation* – Wherever possible, indicate several alternatives and then point out the reasons you selected the best one
3. *Failing to indicate follow up* – Whenever your answer indicates action on your part, make certain that you will take proper follow-up action to see how successful your recommendations, procedures or actions turn out to be
4. *Taking too long in answering any single question* – Remember to time your answers properly

IX. AFTER THE TEST

Scoring procedures differ in detail among civil service jurisdictions although the general principles are the same. Whether the papers are hand-scored or graded by machine we have described, they are nearly always graded by number. That is, the person who marks the paper knows only the number – never the name – of the applicant. Not until all the papers have been graded will they be matched with names. If other tests, such as training and experience or oral interview ratings have been given, scores will be combined. Different parts of the examination usually have different weights. For example, the written test might count 60 percent of the final grade, and a rating of training and experience 40 percent. In many jurisdictions, veterans will have a certain number of points added to their grades.

After the final grade has been determined, the names are placed in grade order and an eligible list is established. There are various methods for resolving ties between those who get the same final grade – probably the most common is to place first the name of the person whose application was received first. Job offers are made from the eligible list in the order the names appear on it. You will be notified of your grade and your rank as soon as all these computations have been made. This will be done as rapidly as possible.

People who are found to meet the requirements in the announcement are called "eligibles." Their names are put on a list of eligible candidates. An eligible's chances of getting a job depend on how high he stands on this list and how fast agencies are filling jobs from the list.

When a job is to be filled from a list of eligibles, the agency asks for the names of people on the list of eligibles for that job. When the civil service commission receives this request, it sends to the agency the names of the three people highest on this list. Or, if the job to be filled has specialized requirements, the office sends the agency the names of the top three persons who meet these requirements from the general list.

The appointing officer makes a choice from among the three people whose names were sent to him. If the selected person accepts the appointment, the names of the others are put back on the list to be considered for future openings.

That is the rule in hiring from all kinds of eligible lists, whether they are for typist, carpenter, chemist, or something else. For every vacancy, the appointing officer has his choice of any one of the top three eligibles on the list. This explains why the person whose name is on top of the list sometimes does not get an appointment when some of the persons lower on the list do. If the appointing officer chooses the second or third eligible, the No. 1 eligible does not get a job at once, but stays on the list until he is appointed or the list is terminated.

X. HOW TO PASS THE INTERVIEW TEST

The examination for which you applied requires an oral interview test. You have already taken the written test and you are now being called for the interview test – the final part of the formal examination.

You may think that it is not possible to prepare for an interview test and that there are no procedures to follow during an interview. Our purpose is to point out some things you can do in advance that will help you and some good rules to follow and pitfalls to avoid while you are being interviewed.

What is an interview supposed to test?

The written examination is designed to test the technical knowledge and competence of the candidate; the oral is designed to evaluate intangible qualities, not readily measured otherwise, and to establish a list showing the relative fitness of each candidate – as measured against his competitors – for the position sought. Scoring is not on the basis of "right" and "wrong," but on a sliding scale of values ranging from "not passable" to "outstanding." As a matter of fact, it is possible to achieve a relatively low score without a single "incorrect" answer because of evident weakness in the qualities being measured.

Occasionally, an examination may consist entirely of an oral test – either an individual or a group oral. In such cases, information is sought concerning the technical knowledges and abilities of the candidate, since there has been no written examination for this purpose. More commonly, however, an oral test is used to supplement a written examination.

Who conducts interviews?

The composition of oral boards varies among different jurisdictions. In nearly all, a representative of the personnel department serves as chairman. One of the members of the board may be a representative of the department in which the candidate would work. In some cases, "outside experts" are used, and, frequently, a businessman or some other representative of the general public is asked to serve. Labor and management or other special groups may be represented. The aim is to secure the services of experts in the appropriate field.

However the board is composed, it is a good idea (and not at all improper or unethical) to ascertain in advance of the interview who the members are and what groups they represent. When you are introduced to them, you will have some idea of their backgrounds and interests, and at least you will not stutter and stammer over their names.

What should be done before the interview?

While knowledge about the board members is useful and takes some of the surprise element out of the interview, there is other preparation which is more substantive. It *is* possible to prepare for an oral interview – in several ways:

1) Keep a copy of your application and review it carefully before the interview

This may be the only document before the oral board, and the starting point of the interview. Know what education and experience you have listed there, and the sequence and dates of all of it. Sometimes the board will ask you to review the highlights of your experience for them; you should not have to hem and haw doing it.

2) Study the class specification and the examination announcement

Usually, the oral board has one or both of these to guide them. The qualities, characteristics or knowledges required by the position sought are stated in these documents. They offer valuable clues as to the nature of the oral interview. For example, if the job involves supervisory responsibilities, the announcement will usually indicate that knowledge of modern supervisory methods and the qualifications of the candidate as a supervisor will be tested. If so, you can expect such questions, frequently in the form of a hypothetical situation which you are expected to solve. NEVER go into an oral without knowledge of the duties and responsibilities of the job you seek.

3) Think through each qualification required

Try to visualize the kind of questions you would ask if you were a board member. How well could you answer them? Try especially to appraise your own knowledge and background in each area, *measured against the job sought*, and identify any areas in which you are weak. Be critical and realistic – do not flatter yourself.

4) Do some general reading in areas in which you feel you may be weak

For example, if the job involves supervision and your past experience has NOT, some general reading in supervisory methods and practices, particularly in the field of human relations, might be useful. Do NOT study agency procedures or detailed manuals. The oral board will be testing your understanding and capacity, not your memory.

5) Get a good night's sleep and watch your general health and mental attitude

You will want a clear head at the interview. Take care of a cold or any other minor ailment, and of course, no hangovers.

What should be done on the day of the interview?

Now comes the day of the interview itself. Give yourself plenty of time to get there. Plan to arrive somewhat ahead of the scheduled time, particularly if your appointment is in the fore part of the day. If a previous candidate fails to appear, the board might be ready for you a bit early. By early afternoon an oral board is almost invariably behind schedule if there are many candidates, and you may have to wait. Take along a book or magazine to read, or your application to review, but leave any extraneous material in the waiting room when you go in for your interview. In any event, relax and compose yourself.

The matter of dress is important. The board is forming impressions about you – from your experience, your manners, your attitude, and your appearance. Give your personal appearance careful attention. Dress your best, but not your flashiest. Choose conservative, appropriate clothing, and be sure it is immaculate. This is a business interview, and your appearance should indicate that you regard it as such. Besides, being well groomed and properly dressed will help boost your confidence.

Sooner or later, someone will call your name and escort you into the interview room. *This is it.* From here on you are on your own. It is too late for any more preparation. But remember, you asked for this opportunity to prove your fitness, and you are here because your request was granted.

What happens when you go in?

The usual sequence of events will be as follows: The clerk (who is often the board stenographer) will introduce you to the chairman of the oral board, who will introduce you to the other members of the board. Acknowledge the introductions before you sit down. Do not be surprised if you find a microphone facing you or a stenotypist sitting by. Oral interviews are usually recorded in the event of an appeal or other review.

Usually the chairman of the board will open the interview by reviewing the highlights of your education and work experience from your application – primarily for the benefit of the other members of the board, as well as to get the material into the record. Do not interrupt or comment unless there is an error or significant misinterpretation; if that is the case, do not hesitate. But do not quibble about insignificant matters. Also, he will usually ask you some question about your education, experience or your present job – partly to get you to start talking and to establish the interviewing "rapport." He may start the actual questioning, or turn it over to one of the other members. Frequently, each member undertakes the questioning on a particular area, one in which he is perhaps most competent, so you can expect each member to participate in the examination. Because time is limited, you may also expect some rather abrupt switches in the direction the questioning takes, so do not be upset by it. Normally, a board member will not pursue a single line of questioning unless he discovers a particular strength or weakness.

After each member has participated, the chairman will usually ask whether any member has any further questions, then will ask you if you have anything you wish to add. Unless you are expecting this question, it may floor you. Worse, it may start you off on an extended, extemporaneous speech. The board is not usually seeking more information. The question is principally to offer you a last opportunity to present further qualifications or to indicate that you have nothing to add. So, if you feel that a significant qualification or characteristic has been overlooked, it is proper to point it out in a sentence or so. Do not compliment the board on the thoroughness of their examination – they have been sketchy, and you know it. If you wish, merely say, "No thank you, I have nothing further to add." This is a point where you can "talk yourself out" of a good impression or fail to present an important bit of information. Remember, *you close the interview yourself.*

The chairman will then say, "That is all, Mr. ______, thank you." Do not be startled; the interview is over, and quicker than you think. Thank him, gather your belongings and take your leave. Save your sigh of relief for the other side of the door.

How to put your best foot forward

Throughout this entire process, you may feel that the board individually and collectively is trying to pierce your defenses, seek out your hidden weaknesses and embarrass and confuse you. Actually, this is not true. They are obliged to make an appraisal of your qualifications for the job you are seeking, and they want to see you in your best light. Remember, they must interview all candidates and a non-cooperative candidate may become a failure in spite of their best efforts to bring out his qualifications. Here are 15 suggestions that will help you:

1) Be natural – Keep your attitude confident, not cocky

If you are not confident that you can do the job, do not expect the board to be. Do not apologize for your weaknesses, try to bring out your strong points. The board is interested in a positive, not negative, presentation. Cockiness will antagonize any board member and make him wonder if you are covering up a weakness by a false show of strength.

2) Get comfortable, but don't lounge or sprawl

Sit erectly but not stiffly. A careless posture may lead the board to conclude that you are careless in other things, or at least that you are not impressed by the importance of the occasion. Either conclusion is natural, even if incorrect. Do not fuss with your clothing, a pencil or an ashtray. Your hands may occasionally be useful to emphasize a point; do not let them become a point of distraction.

3) Do not wisecrack or make small talk

This is a serious situation, and your attitude should show that you consider it as such. Further, the time of the board is limited – they do not want to waste it, and neither should you.

4) Do not exaggerate your experience or abilities

In the first place, from information in the application or other interviews and sources, the board may know more about you than you think. Secondly, you probably will not get away with it. An experienced board is rather adept at spotting such a situation, so do not take the chance.

5) If you know a board member, do not make a point of it, yet do not hide it

Certainly you are not fooling him, and probably not the other members of the board. Do not try to take advantage of your acquaintanceship – it will probably do you little good.

6) Do not dominate the interview

Let the board do that. They will give you the clues – do not assume that you have to do all the talking. Realize that the board has a number of questions to ask you, and do not try to take up all the interview time by showing off your extensive knowledge of the answer to the first one.

7) Be attentive

You only have 20 minutes or so, and you should keep your attention at its sharpest throughout. When a member is addressing a problem or question to you, give him your undivided attention. Address your reply principally to him, but do not exclude the other board members.

8) Do not interrupt

A board member may be stating a problem for you to analyze. He will ask you a question when the time comes. Let him state the problem, and wait for the question.

9) Make sure you understand the question

Do not try to answer until you are sure what the question is. If it is not clear, restate it in your own words or ask the board member to clarify it for you. However, do not haggle about minor elements.

10) Reply promptly but not hastily

A common entry on oral board rating sheets is "candidate responded readily," or "candidate hesitated in replies." Respond as promptly and quickly as you can, but do not jump to a hasty, ill-considered answer.

11) Do not be peremptory in your answers

A brief answer is proper – but do not fire your answer back. That is a losing game from your point of view. The board member can probably ask questions much faster than you can answer them.

12) Do not try to create the answer you think the board member wants

He is interested in what kind of mind you have and how it works – not in playing games. Furthermore, he can usually spot this practice and will actually grade you down on it.

13) Do not switch sides in your reply merely to agree with a board member

Frequently, a member will take a contrary position merely to draw you out and to see if you are willing and able to defend your point of view. Do not start a debate, yet do not surrender a good position. If a position is worth taking, it is worth defending.

14) Do not be afraid to admit an error in judgment if you are shown to be wrong

The board knows that you are forced to reply without any opportunity for careful consideration. Your answer may be demonstrably wrong. If so, admit it and get on with the interview.

15) Do not dwell at length on your present job

The opening question may relate to your present assignment. Answer the question but do not go into an extended discussion. You are being examined for a *new* job, not your present one. As a matter of fact, try to phrase ALL your answers in terms of the job for which you are being examined.

Basis of Rating

Probably you will forget most of these "do's" and "don'ts" when you walk into the oral interview room. Even remembering them all will not ensure you a passing grade. Perhaps you did not have the qualifications in the first place. But remembering them will help you to put your best foot forward, without treading on the toes of the board members.

Rumor and popular opinion to the contrary notwithstanding, an oral board wants you to make the best appearance possible. They know you are under pressure – but they also want to see how you respond to it as a guide to what your reaction would be under the pressures of the job you seek. They will be influenced by the degree of poise you display, the personal traits you show and the manner in which you respond.

ABOUT THIS BOOK

This book contains tests divided into Examination Sections. Go through each test, answering every question in the margin. We have also attached a sample answer sheet at the back of the book that can be removed and used. At the end of each test look at the answer key and check your answers. On the ones you got wrong, look at the right answer choice and learn. Do not fill in the answers first. Do not memorize the questions and answers, but understand the answer and principles involved. On your test, the questions will likely be different from the samples. Questions are changed and new ones added. If you understand these past questions you should have success with any changes that arise. Tests may consist of several types of questions. We have additional books on each subject should more study be advisable or necessary for you. Finally, the more you study, the better prepared you will be. This book is intended to be the last thing you study before you walk into the examination room. Prior study of relevant texts is also recommended. NLC publishes some of these in our Fundamental Series. Knowledge and good sense are important factors in passing your exam. Good luck also helps. So now study this Passbook, absorb the material contained within and take that knowledge into the examination. Then do your best to pass that exam.

EXAMINATION SECTION

EXAMINATION SECTION
TEST 1

DIRECTIONS: Each question or incomplete statement is fol'lowed by several suggested answers or completions. Select the one that BEST answers the question or completes the statement. *PRINT THE LETTER OF THE CORRECT ANSWER IN THE SPACE AT THE RIGHT.*

1. A successful school transportation operation depends MOST upon the high quality of dedication and performance by the 1.____

   A. school administrator
   B. driver
   C. transportation director
   D. supervisor
   E. vehicle maintenance personnel

2. It is NOT the driver's responsibility to 2.____

   A. conduct pre- and post-trip checks on the vehicle
   B. maintain orderly conduct of passengers
   C. communicate effectively with the public
   D. enforce wearing of seatbelts
   E. complete reports

3. The training program for maintenance and service personnel does NOT have to include 3.____

   A. procedure for recognizing cause and effect relationship between driving habits and vehicle maintenance
   B. recovery procedures for vehicles involved in accident or breakdown
   C. preparation of maintenance records
   D. establishment of parts inventory control procedures
   E. repair procedures for each type of vehicle in the fleet

4. A student's riding privileges may be suspended when 4.____

   A. drugs or controlled substances are used on the bus
   B. classroom conduct is not observed on the bus
   C. hazardous materials are brought on the bus
   D. rights of others are jeopardized
   E. safe operation of the bus is jeopardized

5. It is recommended that school officials provide 5.____

   A. clearly marked walkways through the school bus zones
   B. controlled traffic flow through the school bus zones
   C. clearly marked parking patterns through the school bus zones
   D. adequate space for backing of transportation equipment
   E. all of the above

6. What distinguishes a Circular Route? It 6.____

A. is the most economical
B. enables the first student who boards the bus in the morning to be the first to disembark in the evening
C. eliminates the need for students to cross the roadway
D. holds the number of miles a student must ride to a minimum
E. permits one bus to transport more than one load of students

7. Which method for dissemination of information is BEST for informing the public about procedures the schools will follow in cases of severe weather conditions? 7.____

A. Radio
B. Telephone calls
C. Public address system
D. Public press
E. Bulletins

8. What is the BEST method for communicating with students regarding all forms of safety? 8.____

A. Meetings
B. Public address system
C. Bulletins
D. Conference
E. Television

9. Insurance agents should be contacted to determine if additional coverage is necessary when the activity trip is scheduled to 9.____

A. another town
B. another county
C. another state
D. any distance greater than fifty miles
E. any location beyond the school district's boundaries

10. What is the LEAST important factor to be considered in selecting a bus for a trip? 10.____

A. Climate conditions
B. Parking requirements
C. Age group of students
D. Driver familiarity with the route
E. Miles to be traveled

11. Transportation for handicapped students requires an assessment of their ______ capacities. 11.____

A. physical
B. social
C. emotional
D. intellectual
E. all of the above

12. Which of the following is NOT a characteristic of a student with a learning disability? 12.____

A. Average or higher intellectual ability
B. Disorganized in solving problems
C. Demonstrates extreme emotional behaviors
D. Friendly and affectionate
E. Hyperactivity

13. Arrangements for special education students' transportation should be communicated to 13.____

A. parents
B. school personnel
C. other students on the bus
D. the driver
E. all of the above

14. What must be considered to effect behavior modification? 14.____

A. Ages of the students
B. Nature of the reward
C. Clear definition of what constitutes acceptable behavior
D. All of the above
E. None of the above

15. What is the driver's PRIME responsibility when a handicapped student has a seizure? To 15.____

A. administer the student's medication
B. place something in the student's mouth to prevent tongue injury
C. restrain the student's limbs to avoid broken bones
D. see that the student rests comfortably afterward
E. all of the above

16. What is the MOST important preparation for special education student management in an emergency? 16.____

A. Appointing a student to take over
B. Notifying school and parents
C. Reassuring the students
D. Teaching pupils what to expect
E. Preplanning students' needs

17. Suspension of special education students from the bus is usually MOST appropriate when 17.____

A. there is clear evidence of lack of respect for authority
B. the safety of other students is threatened
C. the misbehavior is repeated
D. behavior is drug or alcohol related
E. there is alternate transportation available to the student

18. Which of the following is NOT in the best interest for behavior control? 18.____

A. Rearranging seating positions
B. Relaxing classroom behavioral expectations
C. Suspension of bus privileges
D. Allowing students to suggest and enforce rules
E. Referral to school psychologist

19. Comfort is a HIGH priority when the student has a(n) 19.____

A. visual impairment
B. orthopedic handicap
C. hearing impairment
D. intellectual impairment
E. emotional impairment

20. Facial expression and body language are important aspects in communicating with 20.____

A. the emotionally disturbed
B. the visually handicapped
C. learning disabled students

D. developmentally disabled students
E. hearing impaired students

21. A dry run prior to a scheduled trip date is MOST recommended when 21.____

A. night driving may be involved
B. terrain or road difficulties may be encountered
C. destination parking is other than students' destination
D. bridges or tunnels may be encountered
E. specialized equipment may be used

22. What is the PRIMARY role of the driver transporting handicapped students? To 22.____

A. accommodate student's needs
B. promote successful student management
C. assess and anticipate the needs of individual problems
D. give personal attention to each student
E. drive the bus

23. Who has the FINAL responsibility on an activity bus? 23.____

A. Chaperone
B. Teacher
C. Parent supervisor
D. Senior chaperone
E. Bus driver

24. The Bureau of Motor Carrier Safety Manual recommends which maximum limit for the driver of an activity bus? 24.____

A. ten hours of duty of which eight are driving time
B. ten hours of continuous off-duty prior to a long trip
C. no more than forty hours driving per week
D. no more than sixty hours driving per week
E. twelve hours continuous off-duty prior to a long trip

25. Which of the following is NOT an objective of a planned maintenance program? 25.____

A. Preventing road failures
B. Enhancing appearance of the school bus
C. Improving the handling and performance characteristics
D. Conserving fuel
E. Extending the bus' useful life

KEY (CORRECT ANSWERS)

1.	B	11.	E
2.	D	12.	D
3.	A	13.	E
4.	E	14.	D
5.	A	15.	D
6.	B	16.	E
7.	A	17.	B
8.	B	18.	B
9.	C	19.	B
10.	B	20.	E

21.	B
22.	E
23.	E
24.	D
25.	C

TEST 2

DIRECTIONS: Each question or incomplete statement is followed by several suggested answers or completions. Select the one that BEST answers the question or completes the statement. *PRINT THE LETTER OF THE CORRECT ANSWER IN THE SPACE AT THE RIGHT.*

1. Employee personnel records usually do NOT include 1.____

   A. causes of absences
   B. criminal records
   C. marital status
   D. confirmed work history
   E. psychological evaluation

2. When are alternately flashing red lights used? 2.____

   A. When poor visibility conditions exist
   B. When bus is crossing railroad tracks
   C. When bus is stopping to take on or discharge passengers
   D. When bus is stopped to take on or discharge passengers
   E. All of the above

3. Which of the following policies are determined by state statute and/or state regulations? 3.____

   A. Policy with regard to transportation of non-public school students
   B. Policy relative to supervision of students while loading and unloading at school sites and enroute
   C. Procedure for determining eligibility for student transportation service
   D. Use of special lighting and signaling equipment on the bus
   E. Policy with regard to standees, length of time in transit, and type of supervision required

4. Which of the following is NOT a qualification of the director of student transportation? 4.____

   A. A record free of criminal convictions
   B. An undergraduate degree or equivalent experience
   C. Ability to work effectively with a broad range of individuals
   D. Ability to provide comprehensive bus driver training program
   E. Ability to manage personnel and resources

5. The driver training program SHOULD include instruction in 5.____

   A. repair procedures
   B. recovery procedures for vehicles involved in an accident
   C. procedures for performing pre- and post-trip inspections
   D. preparation of maintenance records
   E. all of the above

6. All of the following are bus regulations regarding student demeanors EXCEPT: 6.____

   A. Students are to remain seated
   B. Students are to place school-related objects in aisles
   C. Students are prohibited from eating on the bus

D. Students are prohibited from leaving or boarding the bus at locations other than assigned home or school stop
E. Students are permitted to pass objects on, from, or into buses

7. Students should be instructed on 7.____

A. proper storage of material that cannot be held on their laps
B. safe eating and drinking procedures on the bus
C. entering and leaving the bus
D. passing objects on, from, or into the bus
E. all of the above

8. Which type route eliminates the need for the student to cross the roadway? 8.____

A. Shoestring route
B. Retracing route
C. Double routing
D. Emergency route
E. Circular route

9. A systemic inspection of the bus before each trip is the responsibility of the 9.____

A. bus garage personnel
B. school administration
C. transportation supervisor
D. driver
E. service and maintenance personnel

10. What is the BEST way to inform parents of all school and state regulations? 10.____

A. Conferences
B. Telephone calls
C. Letters
D. Meetings
E. Radio

11. Safety criteria for evaluating the transportation system usually does NOT include 11.____

A. property damage accidents
B. moving traffic violations
C. complaints
D. route and routing procedures
E. road failures

12. How many days in advance of a trip date should driver assignment take place? ______ day(s). 12.____

A. 7 B. 1 C. 3 D. 2 E. 5

13. Which of the following is NOT a consideration for selecting drivers for trip assignments? 13.____

A. License held
B. Seniority
C. Skill
D. Familiarity with trip vehicle
E. Familiarity with area to be traveled

14. Which group of students does NOT represent any unusual behavior problems? 14.____

A. Developmentally disabled students
B. Learning disabled students
C. Hearing disabled students
D. All of the above
E. None of the above

15. A lack of stability from day to day in desirable behavior is characteristic of _______ students. 15.____

A. emotionally disturbed
B. learning disabled
C. developmentally disabled
D. visually handicapped
E. hearing impaired

16. What type of student is MOST likely to have few self-care skills? _______ students. 16.____

A. Learning disabled
B. Developmentally disabled
C. Emotionally disturbed
D. Orthopedically handicapped
E. Visually handicapped

17. What is the BEST approach to special education students? 17.____

A. Promptly correct any unsuitable behavior
B. Tell rather than show pupils what you want them to do
C. Define rules clearly and enforce them firmly
D. Allow some latitude because of students' handicaps
E. Do not expect students to accept responsibility for their own actions

18. Behavior modification when applied to special education students requires 18.____

A. giving a reward after demonstration of appropriate behavior
B. long-term behavioral goals
C. liberal amounts of praise to encourage acceptable behavior
D. establishing rules that can be easily followed
E. taking appropriate disciplinary action for each rule infraction

19. Which of the following confidential information should the aide on a bus transporting handicapped students have? 19.____

A. Nature of student's handicap
B. Emergency health care information
C. Name and phone number of student's parents
D. All of the above
E. None of the above

20. It is BEST to seat a young and hyperactive special education student 20.____

A. with a very young student
B. at the front of the bus
C. at the rear of the bus
D. with an older, well-behaved student
E. with a fragile student

21. All medically-related incidents involving special education students require 21.____

    A. summoning professional medical attention
    B. the driver to give medication or medical assistance
    C. reporting to school and parents at earliest possible moment
    D. all of the above
    E. none of the above

22. Visually handicapped students respond BEST when 22.____

    A. they are given independence
    B. they are consistently reminded what is expected of them
    C. angry outbursts and punishment is avoided
    D. they are addressed by name
    E. body language is used to reinforce speech

23. What is the LAST consideration in planning for the transportation of special education students? 23.____
The

    A. group of students on the vehicle
    B. design of the car seats
    C. type of supports needed
    D. type of vehicle required
    E. class placement of students

24. The driver of handicapped children needs to be more 24.____

    A. controlled B. alert C. flexible
    D. lenient E. rigid

25. Which of the following is USUALLY necessary when a special trip is planned? 25.____

    A. Bus is equipped with radio
    B. Public address system is installed
    C. Driver is provided with cash
    D. Driver is provided with a uniform
    E. Seats are equipped with seatbelts

KEY (CORRECT ANSWERS)

1. E
2. D
3. A
4. D
5. C

6. B
7. C
8. B
9. D
10. C

11. D
12. C
13. A
14. C
15. A

16. B
17. C
18. A
19. D
20. D

21. C
22. D
23. A
24. C
25. C

EXAMINATION SECTION
TEST 1

DIRECTIONS: Each question or incomplete statement is followed by several suggested answers or completions. Select the one that BEST answers the question or completes the statement. *PRINT THE LETTER OF THE CORRECT ANSWER IN THE SPACE AT THE RIGHT.*

1. Pick-up and delivery points in suburban districts should include the following EXCEPT: 1_____

   A. Corner pick-ups at traffic-controlled locations should be discouraged
   B. Young passengers should cross streets at locations where protection is a community responsibility
   C. There should be minimum interference with traffic on arterial or collector streets
   D. Area discharge points away from the heavy traffic should be designated
   E. Personalized bus stops should not be permitted

2. The success of safety programs depends on involvement beginning at the _______ level. 2_____

   A. county
   B. state
   C. district
   D. individual
   E. national

3. Fleet accidents and costs are MOST affected by 3_____

   A. bus selection and equipment
   B. operating maintenance policies
   C. driver attitude
   D. bus routes and fleet utilization
   E. the fleets public image

4. Which of the following is the LEAST important consideration concerning the hiring of low I.Q. drivers? 4_____

   A. Lack of accurate judgment in emergency situations
   B. Difficulty in concentrating while driving a vehicle
   C. Make poor witnesses in cases of accident
   D. Difficult to supervise
   E. Difficulty taking decisive action

5. How does the supervisor evaluate the trainees' progress? By 5_____

   A. *evaluating* written test scores
   B. *observing* attitudes and safety awareness
   C. *observing* driver performance over a prescribed course
   D. *observing* driver's performance while transportingpupils
   E. *evaluating* the results of driving simulation tests

6. What type of driver testing is needed to enable the supervisor to help each driver develop the compensating habits needed to drive safely? _______ test. 6_____

   A. Reaction time
   B. Distance judgment
   C. Visual
   D. Tunnel vision
   E. Glare recovery

7. *Protection Routes* do NOT usually consider 7_____

A. traffic volume on available alternate routes
B. railroad crossings
C. distance to be traveled
D. sharp curves
E. narrow pavements

8. Policy statements from the local school board should define all the following EXCEPT: 8_____

A. Minimum requirements for driver selection and training
B. The extent of school bus service
C. Factual basis for establishing transportation policies
D. Equipment replacement schedule
E. Provisions for extracurricular transportation

9. Driver selection, training, and motivation MUST be designed to 9_____

A. get and keep uniform standards of vehicle operation
B. transport and supervise students
C. the principles of defensive driving
D. prevent accidents
E. develop responsibility

10. What is the MOST important quality for a school bus driver? 10_____

A. Physical fitness
B. Congenial personality
C. High intelligence
D. Neat appearance
E. Emotional maturity

11. Drivers who complete an initial training course usually do NOT know 11_____

A. the laws and regulations applicable to school bus fleet operation
B. how to administer first aid
C. the flexibility of schedules
D. how to deal with students who disobey rules
E. how to operate a fire extinguisher

12. Which of the following motivational methods and techniques are recommended for use by supervisors? 12_____

A. Terminate the employ of any driver involved in a preventable accident
B. Hold driver responsible for cleanliness of bus
C. Do not publicly single out individuals for merit
D. Do not inform drivers of the high degree of skill required before qualifying to drive in the fleet
E. Defuse any developing spirit of competitiveness

13. Remedial training is PRIMARILY intended to instruct 13_____

A. operation of new equipment
B. changes in policies, laws, and regulations
C. problem drivers
D. older drivers
E. new drivers with previous driving experience

14. Glare recovery is an important test for anyone who drives when 14____

A. there is strong sunlight
B. the roads are snow-covered
C. headlights must be used
D. the roads are slick with rain
E. routes involve tunnels

15. When does driver instruction begin? With the 15____

A. first training class
B. introduction to the vehicle
C. orientation session
D. first road test
E. first contact with the supervisor

16. Which of the following factors MOST contributes to triggering accidents? 16____

A. Weather conditions
B. Road conditions
C. Condition of vehicle
D. Driving errors
E. Student behavior

17. School bus drivers may continue to drive if they have suffered the loss of 17____

A. a finger
B. a hand
C. a foot
D. all of the above
E. none of the above

18. Which of the following would NOT bar a person from driving a school bus? 18____

A. Impaired use of foot or leg
B. Any disease likely to interfere with safe driving
C. Use of alcohol beverages
D. Impaired use of arm or hand
E. Addiction of habit-forming drugs

19. What factor determines the safety and efficiency of the school transportation program? 19____

A. The vehicle
B. The driver
C. The maintenance of the vehicle
D. All of the above
E. None of the above

20. Violations of traffic laws CANNOT be condoned because they 20____

A. cause loss of respect by motorists for school vehicles
B. may result in reduced use of public streets
C. may expose pupils to serious hazards
D. increase the cost of school transportation
E. reflect badly on the school system

21. What state department is MOST directly responsible for student transportation? 21____

A. Transportation
B. Motor vehicles
C. Public welfare
D. Public safety
E. Education

22. What is the MOST important consideration to be included in the specifications for new vehicle purchases? 22____

A. Ages of pupils to be transported
B. Type of terrain in which vehicle will be used
C. The pattern of transit operation
D. The fleets1 safety performance
E. The activities for which the vehicle will be used

23. What MOST motivates drivers to perform safely? 23____

A. Recognition and appreciation by the school district
B. Attendance at safety seminars
C. Policy of rapid dismissal of unsafe drivers
D. Proper pupil behavior
E. The operating condition of the vehicle

24. All of the following are responsibilities of the school superintendent EXCEPT: 24____

A. Show interest in good accident control program
B. Outline responsibilities of all participants in the transportation system
C. Provide specific guidelines for driver recruitment and training
D. Establish standards for bus maintenance
E. Involve schools and parents in transportation safety program

25. Which of the following is NOT an indication of substandard driver performance? 25____

A. Inadequate maintenance
B. Errors in the performance of work
C. Changes in everyday behavior and manners
D. Near accidents
E. Changes in simple habits of a routine nature

KEY (CORRECT ANSWERS)

1. A
2. B
3. B
4. B
5. C
6. D
7. C
8. C
9. D
10. E
11. A
12. B
13. C
14. C
15. E
16. D
17. A
18. C
19. D
20. C
21. E
22. B
23. A
24. D
25. A

TEST 2

DIRECTIONS: Each question or incomplete statement is followed by several suggested answers or completions. Select the one that BEST answers the question or completes the statement. *PRINT THE LETTER OF THE CORRECT ANSWER IN THE SPACE AT THE RIGHT.*

1. Who should be responsible for driver selection? 1____

   A. District superintendent
   B. Transportation supervisor
   C. School office of personnel
   D. School board
   E. Contractor

2. Which of the following is LEAST important regarding the school bus driver? Driver 2____

   A. finds satisfaction in job
   B. gets along well with others
   C. is courteous to pedestrians and motorists
   D. is highly intelligent
   E. has neat appearance

3. What is the MOST important ingredient in an efficient school transportation service? 3____

   A. Safe driving
   B. Control of students
   C. Safe bus routes
   D. Vehicle maintenance
   E. Compliance with traffic regulations

4. The amount of time needed for initial training depends on the 4____

   A. person employed
   B. selection program
   C. person's experience
   D. all of the above
   E. none of the above

5. What is the purpose of refresher training? To 5____

   A. develop an appreciation of the importance of the job
   B. keep performance efficient and safe
   C. prevent accidents
   D. solves problems
   E. evaluate physical fitness of older drivers

6. What is the key to the success of a safety program? 6____

   A. Driver selection
   B. Supervision
   C. Maintenance
   D. Money
   E. Driver motivation

7. What instruction technique is MOST useful for remedial training? 7____

   A. Individual reading material
   B. Classroom lecture

C. Road instruction
D. Videotape
E. Group discussion

8. What is the emphasis of reaction time testing? The 8_____

A. importance of keeping an adequate distance between moving vehicles
B. time needed to react to an emergency situation or condition
C. ability to evaluate distance
D. ability to estimate the speed of approaching vehicles
E. development of compensating habits

9. Eighty percent of the total number of accidents annually involve 9_____

A. single cars
B. car/truck collisions
C. two cars
D. multiple cars
E. multiple trucks

10. All of the following are proper backing procedures EXCEPT: 10_____

A. get out of bus before beginning to back
B. backing from the passenger's side
C. using a reliable person for guidance
D. check both sides continually while backing
E. backing slowly

11. Minimum visual acuity in both eyes with or without glasses should NOT be less than (Snellen) 11_____

A. 15/20 B. 20/20 C. 20/40 D. 20/60 E. 20/200

12. Which of the following is NOT a disqualifying condition for school bus drivers? 12_____

A. Diabetes
B. Cardiovascular disease
C. Hernia
D. Pregnancy
E. Back injury

13. What MOST determines the size requirement of the driver? 13_____

A. Type of students to be transported
B. Federal regulations
C. Configuration of the driver's compartment
D. Height of bus
E. Type of bus

14. The catalyst to the safety and efficiency of the school bus transportation program is the 14_____

A. local school board
B. driver
C. student
D. district supervisor
E. safety supervisor

15. In order to prepare specifications for bus purchases, what should the safety supervisor know? 15_____

A. Knowledge of bus routes
B. Knowledge of students to be transported

C. Knowledge of environmental conditions
D. Knowledge of operational conditions
E. All of the above

16. Which of the following necessitates the planning of *Protection Routes?* 16_____

A. Scattered pick-up locations
B. Inclement weather conditions
C. Transportation of students outside the community
D. Unexpected traffic delays
E. Transportation of special education students

17. What qualification would MOST recommend a pupil to the position of bus monitor? 17_____

A. Height and weight
B. Intelligence
C. Maturity
D. Lives near start of bus line
E. Lives near end of bus line

18. What is the MOST important criteria in adopting management for the special education student? 18_____

A. Selecting the proper driver
B. Behavior modification
C. Providing personalized service
D. Planning for each student's needs prior to placement
E. Providing comfortable transportation

19. All activity trips should require the presence of 19_____

A. adult chaperone
B. teacher
C. school official
D. parent
E. all of the above

20. Under what conditions may loose luggage or equipment be transported in the passenger compartment of an activity bus? 20_____

A. When there is no danger of causing injury
B. When it does not block passageways
C. When the destination is a league sporting event
D. When it can be safely secured
E. None of the above

21. Which of the following items should be carried on the bus at all times? 21_____

A. Instant camera for scene report
B. Cards for witness signatures
C. Portable, tape recorder for witness testimony
D. Radio to summon help
E. All of the above

22. An operational plan to provide two-way communication with parents is imperative in the event of 22____

A. sudden disability of driver
B. road failure
C. strikes by school staff or drivers
D. accident
E. civil defense drill

23. When are standees permitted while the bus is in motion? 23____

A. When written permission is obtained
B. During special activity trips
C. When safety straps are provided
D. All of the above
E. None of the above

24. Statistics show that automobile accidents occur MOST frequently 24____

A. in the morning rush hours
B. around noon
C. soon after sunset
D. near midnight
E. just before sunrise

25. A bus driver is liable under the law to receive a traffic ticket for 25____

A. double standing when a bus stop is occupied by a car
B. not taking on all people waiting at a stop
C. passing a preceding bus on a grade
D. discharging a passenger at other than a bus stop
E. none of the above

KEY (CORRECT ANSWERS)

1. B
2. D
3. A
4. D
5. B
6. E
7. E
8. A
9. C
10. B
11. C
12. D
13. C
14. E
15. E
16. C
17. C
18. D
19. A
20. E
21. B
22. D
23. E
24. C
25. D

TEST 3

DIRECTIONS: Each question or incomplete statement is followed by several suggested answers or completions. Select the one that BEST answers the question or completes the statement. *PRINT THE LETTER OF THE CORRECT ANSWER IN THE SPACE AT THE RIGHT.*

1. A transportation director who rides the school bus is NOT required to observe 1_____

   A. the conditions at the school's loading and unloading areas
   B. operation of vehicle in accordance with prescribed regulations
   C. accuracy of driver!s route and schedule
   D. driver-student ratio
   E. driver attitude toward other motorists and pedestrians

2. Which of the following would be proper procedure for conducting an emergency drill? 2_____

   A. Student may exit with lunchboxes and books.
   B. The driver should assist the students out of the bus.
   C. Drills should be held on the actual bus route.
   D. Drills should be held more often in the spring and fall.
   E. Students who ride buses on special trips may be excluded.

3. What is the goal in planning the parking of buses at the school loading zone? To 3_____

   A. accommodate the maximum number of buses
   B. exclude the necessity for backing up the buses
   C. inhibit the regular flow of traffic within the school site
   D. achieve the closest proximity to the school building
   E. accommodate student pick-up by parents

4. No portion of the bus may be driven onto railroad tracks if the view in either direction is obstructed for _______ feet. 4_____

   A. 250 B. 100 C. 2000 D. 500 E. 1000

5. A fleet's safety performance should measure the number of accidents per 5_____

   A. vehicle within a year
   B. vehicle mile within a year
   C. vehicle within a month
   D. length route and students carried
   E. vehicle mile within a month

6. Bus drills used to teach students about emergency evacuation procedures should have everyone exit through the 6_____

   A. front entrance door
   B. rear emergency door
   C. emergency window
   D. front entrance door or rear emergency door
   E. rear emergency door or emergency window

7. What sign or signal may be activated from the bus while it is stopped for a railroad crossing? 7_____

A. Stop signal arm
B. White flashing strobe light
C. Yellow signal lamps
D. Red signal lamps
E. Turn signal lights

8. The driver must evacuate the bus if in normal traffic conditions the bus is not visible for a MINIMUM distance of _______ feet. 8_____

A. 1000 B. 50 C. 300 D. 100 E. 500

9. What is the MINIMUM radius on the inner edge of pavement on all road curves within the school site? _______ feet. 9_____

A. 50 B. 100 C. 60 D. 80 E. 90

10. All of the following are recommended EXCEPT: 10_____

A. Roads should completely encircle a school
B. Curbing should be constructed on all roads
C. Eliminate all crossroads in front of buses
D. A maximum standard of 5% grade is allowed on all roads
E. Traffic control devices should be provided at all exits

11. Under what condition may a driver NOT proceed across railroad tracks unless authorized by a law enforcement officer or flagman? 11_____

A. Tracks at which there is in operation any flashing red lights and/or bell
B. During wet, stormy, or foggy weather
C. Tracks controlled by crossing gate or barrier
D. Tracks at which there is a railroad grade crossing
E. Tracks not controlled by traffic signals

12. What is the SAFEST way to proceed if a bus stops near a precipice where it could still move and go over the cliff? 12_____

A. Instruct students to remain in seats
B. Redistribute carrying weight of students to area of greatest stability
C. Driver should exit and stabilize bus with emergency equipment
D. Instruct students to assume *crash* position
E. Evacuate bus

13. Which of the following would NOT necessitate the evacuation of a school bus? 13_____

A. Danger of fire
B. Behavior control
C. Unsafe position
D. All of the above
E. None of the above

14. How far from the bus should students go during an emergency drill? _______ feet. 14_____

A. 100 B. 300 C. 25 D. 50 E. 200

15. Bus canopies have been found to be advantageous in 15_____

A. schools with handicapped students
B. elementary schools

C. schools with large enrollments
D. schools with small enrollments
E. schools located in cold climates

16. How far from rails nearest the front of the bus must the driver come to a complete stop? _______ feet. 16____

A. 25 B. 15 C. 50 D. 35 E. 60

17. Which of the following factors pertaining to school bus evacuation must be considered FIRST? 17____

A. Safety of students
B. Stability of vehicle
C. Leadership capacity of driver
D. Communication of emergency situation to proper authority
E. Maturity of students

18. What is the SAFEST way to park buses for loading and unloading? 18____

A. Perpendicular to curb, front end facing
B. Perpendicular to curb, rear end facing
C. Diagonal to curb, front end facing
D. Diagonal to curb, rear end facing
E. Bumper to bumper, alongside curb

19. Diagonal parking requires a MINIMUM width of paved surface of _______ feet. 19____

A. 50 B. 60 C. 30 D. 100 E. 40

20. When the bus driver is incapacitated, it is NOT necessary for the appointed student monitor to know how to 20____

A. turn off ignition switch
B. set emergency brake
C. use the fire ax
D. set flags and flares
E. put transmission in gear

21. If it is necessary to load or unload students on the main thoroughfare in front of the school, a paved road should be provided at least _______ feet wide. 21____

A. 36 B. 24 C. 48 D. 60 E. 40

22. What MINIMUM tangent section should be provided between reverse curves? _______ feet. 22____

A. 60 B. 50 C. 30 D. 40 E. 75

23. During an evacuation drill, the 23____

A. ignition should be left off
B. transmission should be in neutral position
C. front entrance door should be blocked
D. emergency doors' folding stirrup step should be used
E. all of the above

24. What is the MAXIMUM standard of grade allowed for roads on school sites? 24_____

A. 1% B. 5% C. 2% D. 7% E. 3%

25. School bus safety is BEST achieved when 25_____

A. separate loading zones accommodate two-way bus traffic
B. intersections within school site are eliminated
C. trees and shrubbery are not planted or eliminated
D. island construction in driveways should be avoided
E. all roads should be of uniform width

KEY (CORRECT ANSWERS)

1. D
2. D
3. B
4. E
5. B
6. D
7. E
8. C
9. C
10. A
11. A
12. E
13. B
14. A
15. A
16. C
17. A
18. C
19. B
20. E
21. E
22. B
23. A
24. B
25. B

EXAMINATION SECTION
TEST 1

DIRECTIONS: Each question or incomplete statement is followed by several suggested answers or completions. Select the one that BEST answers the question or completes the statement. *PRINT THE LETTER OF THE CORRECT ANSWER IN THE SPACE AT THE RIGHT.*

1. Which of the following types of services is MOST likely to involve overtime pay for operators? 1.____

   A. Special education
   B. Extracurricular
   C. Regular home-to-school service
   D. Desegregation

2. In making cost estimates, it is important to separate mechanics' wages and other mechanical, fuel, and repair costs in terms of the ______ each type of service. 2.____

   A. individual personnel conducting
   B. number of miles for
   C. overall monthly departmental consumption of
   D. individual vehicle used for

3. Which of the following is most likely to be used as a measure of the efficiency of the use of buses by a transportation department? 3.____

   A. Percentage of vehicle capacity used at each route's peak period
   B. Stops per 1,000 vehicle miles
   C. Number of students transported by each bus per route
   D. Ratio of students transported to miles driven

4. Performance measures among transportation departments are typically used for each of the following EXCEPT as a(n) 4.____

   A. objective yardstick for evaluating the service being provided
   B. basis for comparison with other departments with similar variables
   C. basis for monitoring a contractor's compliance with the terms of a contract
   D. basis for recognizing or sanctioning employees

5. Which of the following is an example of a direct cost that would be calculated by route or type of service? 5.____

   A. Cost of capital
   B. Bus depreciation
   C. Collision insurance
   D. Fuel costs

6. If a contractor is responsible for the operation of transportation services, it is customary to require that the contractor maintain fleet records for a minimum of ______, at no cost to the district or school. 6.____

   A. 90 days
   B. 6 months
   C. 1 year
   D. 5 years

7. If a district decides to increase the maximum time spent on buses by students, the most likely effect would be a(n) 7.____

A. increase in operating costs
B. shortening of the walking radius
C. increase in the number of bus routes
D. increase in the size of the service area

8. If a transportation department purchases buses outright or lease-purchases them, the cash expense is typically realized in ______ year(s). 8.____

A. 1 B. 1-2 C. 3-5 D. 5-10

9. If more than one educational agency wants to enter into an interagency agreement that will allow each organization to make capital investments, the best form of administration for their transportation services would be 9.____

A. in-lieu payments
B. a joint power authority
C. a loose consortium
D. a cooperative

10. Each of the following is an example of a direct cost to the transportation department that cannot be identified directly with a particular type of route or service EXCEPT 10.____

A. operators' overtime premiums
B. liability insurance
C. purchased vehicle maintenance services
D. bus lease costs

11. A filing system on bus operators should usually include a tickler file that indicates those drivers who should be evaluated within the next 11.____

A. 14 days B. 30 days C. 3 months D. year

12. In order to accurately estimate the costs of a transportation department, costs data should be collected for a period of at LEAST 12.____

A. 3 months B. 6 months C. 1 year D. 2 years

13. Which of the following is generally NOT true of a school or district which provides all of its own transportation services? 13.____

A. Costs are minimized by the profit motive.
B. The school or district is the agency with sole legal liability.
C. Procurement and personnel processes are lengthy and demanding.
D. Service quality is flexible.

14. Which of the following is a fixed and allocated indirect cost to a transportation department? 14.____

A. Costs of central school services used
B. Fire/property insurance
C. Cost of capital
D. Utilities for terminal and shop

15. In school or district transportation departments, preventive maintenance inspections are typically performed on vehicles every 15.____

A. 30 days
B. 3,000 miles or 45 days, whichever comes first
C. 5,000 miles
D. 7,500 miles or 6 months, whichever comes first

16. Which of the following is NOT considered to be a general performance measure used by a transportation department? 16.____

A. Compliments or complaints
B. Percentage of vehicle capacity used
C. Vehicle downtime
D. Stops or runs missed

17. A district decides to transfer the responsibility for operating its transportation services to an outside contractor. In order to be fair to its current operators and to the contractor, the district should require 17.____

A. a lump-sum buyout by the contractor of any of the district's current bus drivers who are not hired by the contractor
B. that the contractor agree to interview for bus driver positions all drivers currently serving the district who request interviews
C. a reduction in the overall number of drivers used to meet the requirements of newly-designed routes
D. that the contractor hire all drivers currently serving the district who request to be hired

18. In measuring the performance of a particular bus route, most departments consider a bus to be *late* 18.____

A. if it shows up within any period, however, small, past the scheduled arrival
B. if it arrives at a stop more than 15 minutes after it was scheduled to arrive
C. *only* if it arrives at its final destination with a margin of fewer than 15 minutes remaining before the start of the first scheduled class or activity
D. *only* if students miss a portion of the activity or class to which the bus is delivering them

19. Cooperatives, consortiums, or multilateral interagency agreements for providing transportation services are likely to involve 19.____

A. a strict interagency hierarchy
B. more economical insurance coverage
C. greater accountability to school or district administrators
D. a higher level of managerial oversight

Questions 20-21.

DIRECTIONS: Questions 20 and 21 refer to the following information. A personnel department can determine the total hours worked by bus operators, but does not know the separate wage cost for each type of service.

20. What is the cost category that should be used in the above problem? 20.____

A. Ratio of operators' wages to miles driven
B. Operators' wages for hours worked
C. Miles driven
D. Hours of bus service

21. What is the allocation factor in the above problem? 21.____

A. Ratio of operators' wages to miles driven
B. Operators' wages for hours worked
C. Miles driven
D. Hours of bus service

22. When used as a performance measure, statistics on non-collision injury incidents associated with transportation services are typically calculated in incidents corresponding to 22.____

A. 1,000 miles driven per bus
B. 1,000 wage hours per operator
C. 1,000 pupils transported per month
D. one million vehicle miles

23. Schools or districts considering a contracting arrangement for transportation services are most likely to overlook 23.____

A. management and labor costs of writing a request for proposals (RFP) and contract
B. avoidable costs of school or district delivery
C. salary and benefit costs of a contract administrator position
D. material costs of writing a request for proposals (RFP) and contract

24. Which of the following is NOT a necessary factor in computing the training wage costs for a transportation department? 24.____

A. The number of drivers attending
B. Number of non-training hours worked
C. Hourly wages
D. The number of training hours received

25. Which of the following is/are summary measures of the overall efficiency of a pupil transportation operation? 25.____

I. Direct variable costs to the department per mile for all types of services
II. Full cost per mile, including both live and deadhead miles
III. Transportation department overhead costs per pupil transported
IV. Full cost per pupil transported each way, each day

The CORRECT answer is:

A. I, II
B. II, IV
C. II, III, IV
D. I, II, III

KEY (CORRECT ANSWERS)

1.	B	11.	B
2.	D	12.	C
3.	A	13.	A
4.	B	14.	A
5.	D	15.	B
6.	C	16.	C
7.	D	17.	B
8.	C	18.	C
9.	B	19.	B
10.	C	20.	B

21.	D
22.	C
23.	C
24.	B
25.	B

TEST 2

DIRECTIONS: Each question or incomplete statement is followed by several suggested answers or completions. Select the one that BEST answers the question or completes the statement. *PRINT THE LETTER OF THE CORRECT ANSWER IN THE SPACE AT THE RIGHT.*

1. Which of the following credentials would NOT be part of the records needed to satisfy most state requirements for bus drivers? 1.____

   A. Driver training record card
   B. Evidence of first aid
   C. Negative tuberculin test evidence
   D. Class C or non-commercial driver's license

2. Agencies with students who live in remote areas may choose a payment-in-lieu-of-services arrangement rather than deliver transportation services. An agency engaged in such an arrangement should expect it to involve 2.____

   A. strict accountability standards for parents
   B. high day-to-day involvement in managing
   C. continued liability for pupil safety
   D. payment on a per-pupil basis

3. The most difficult costs for a transportation department to measure are typically 3.____

   A. purchased vehicle maintenance services
   B. rent, lease or depreciation costs for land and buildings used
   C. central school or district services used by the department
   D. depreciation, lease, or rental costs for buses

4. The performance measure most often used among transportation departments for workers' compensation claims is the 4.____

   A. number of claims per 100 employees per year
   B. number of claims per route per year
   C. number of claims per year in excess of $500
   D. total number of claims per year

5. The primary advantage associated with using longer-term contracts for the provision of transportation services is 5.____

   A. greater flexibility
   B. fewer disagreements with contractor
   C. more competitive bidding
   D. liability exposure is usually increased for the district or department

6. When used as performance measures in transportation departments, safety-related statistics are usually calculated in units corresponding to 6.____

   A. 1,000 miles driven per bus
   B. 1,000 pupils transported per month
   C. 1,000 operator's wage hours
   D. one million vehicle miles

7. A school district is considering whether to turn the administration of its transportation services over to an outside contractor. Before any comparison of the district's current cost of services or capital can be fairly compared to those of a contractor, it will be necessary to 7.____

   A. consider at least three competitive bids
   B. subtract nonavoidable costs from the full cost of the district's service or item of capital
   C. separate fixed from variable costs and determine whether the contractor's costs are similarly fixed or variable
   D. compare amortization tables used in determining the cost of capital items

8. For a transportation department which makes use of contractors, it is generally most important for the district to retain authority over 8.____

   A. routing and scheduling
   B. vehicle maintenance
   C. operations and dispatch
   D. driver training

9. During the process of bidding for the provision of transportation services, it is customary for a proposer to be forbidden from withdrawing his bid for a period of ______ days after the date set for the receipt of bid proposals. 9.____

   A. 10
   B. 30
   C. 60
   D. 90

10. Multiplying the book value of an item of transportation-related equipment by the interest rate paid by a school or district when it borrows money will yield the 10.____

    A. indirect costs of transportation
    B. cost of capital
    C. variable costs
    D. amortization rate

11. Which of the following is most likely to be true of a bilateral interagency agreement for the provision of pupil transportation? 11.____

    A. Service provision involves more direct accountability than with a single provider.
    B. Fixed costs are often duplicated.
    C. Economies of scale are nearly impossible.
    D. More efficient service than with a single provider

12. Which of the following decisions on the part of a school or district would be most likely to improve cost savings? 12.____

    A. Increasing walking radius
    B. Changing bell schedules
    C. Increasing the use of in-lieu payments
    D. Increasing the area of a route

13. A district, fielding bids from providers of transportation services, decides to accept bids on the basis of the number of hours of service provided. The MAIN advantage to this approach is that 13.____

A. it makes bidding more competitive among proposers
B. proposers do not face a significant risk of unforeseen costs
C. the district will have an easier time monitoring the number of hours of service provided
D. it reduces the number of line-items in a proposal

14. In estimating costs, mechanics' wages for time during shop upkeep, disability, sick leave, or vacation are calculated by 14._____

A. subtracting mechanics' hours per route from total mechanics' wages
B. adding mechanics' wages for hours worked and total mechanics' wages
C. dividing total mechanic's wages by the mechanic's hours for each individual route, then adding up the totals, then subtracting from wages for total hours worked
D. subtracting mechanics' wages for hours worked from total mechanics' wages

15. A school district transports 5,000 students each way daily, on average, over a period of a month. It it receives 10 complaints on bus service during the month of September, what is the *complaint measure* for September? 15._____

A. 2 B. 10 C. 50 D. 500

16. A district has decided to issue an intent to award notice to a contractor who has submitted a bid for the provision of transportation services. Typically, the district will then reserve the right to negotiate changes in the scope of work that do not exceed _______% of the initial price bid. 16._____

A. 5 B. 10 C. 15 D. 20

17. Each of the following is an example of a transportation department's fixed overhead costs EXCEPT 17._____

A. mechanic's overtime premiums
B. operator's overtime premiums
C. terminal support staff salaries and benefits
D. workers' compensation insurance for mechanics

18. In the process of accepting bids for transportation services, a proposer's bond presented by a contractor is typically offered at a rate of _______% of the total bid proposal price. 18._____

A. 5 B. 7 C. 10 D. 15

19. Which of the following decisions on the part of a school or district would be most likely to reduce the number of students served? 19._____

A. Increasing the walking radius
B. Improving the route design
C. Increasing the use of in-lieu payments
D. Redesigning routes

20. Which of the following is/are advantages specific to the administration of transportation services by means of a contract with a private provider? 20.____
    I. The ability to make wholesale changes in the provision of services in a short time
    II. The minimization of costs
    III. Reduced need for quality monitoring
    IV. Lower staff turnover

    The CORRECT answer is:

    A. I, II B. II, III C. III, IV D. I, IV

21. Setting different start times for ______ school(s) is NOT a typical way in which a district may coordinate bell schedules to allow an increased number of runs per bus. 21.____

    A. elementary schools, middle schools, and high
    B. different programs within individual
    C. specific grade levels within individual
    D. each individual

22. In most jurisdictions, a long-term contract with a provider of transportation services may not exist for a term longer than ______ year(s). 22.____

    A. 1 B. 5 C. 10 D. 15

23. Occasionally, a school or district may arrange student transportation with a public carrier. Any agency which engages in such an arrangement should expect it to involve 23.____

    A. a good degree of flexibility in routes and scheduling
    B. a high degree of school or district management attention
    C. a generalized lack of parental comfort
    D. high per-pupil costs

24. Schools or districts considering a contracting arrangement for transportation services should keep in mind that writing a new contract and a request for proposals (RFP) will probably require about ______ hours of management time. 24.____

    A. 20-60 B. 40-100 C. 50-150 D. 120-200

25. In an arrangement in which a district requires a contractor to use a district-owned terminal, which will typically be easiest for the district to monitor? 25.____

    A. Portal-to-portal miles
    B. Total miles
    C. Live hours
    D. Per-pupil ridership

KEY (CORRECT ANSWERS)

1.	D	11.	D
2.	C	12.	B
3.	B	13.	B
4.	A	14.	D
5.	C	15.	A
6.	D	16.	B
7.	B	17.	B
8.	A	18.	A
9.	C	19.	A
10.	B	20.	A

21. C
22. B
23. C
24. C
25. A

EXAMINATION SECTION
TEST 1

DIRECTIONS: Each question or incomplete statement is followed by several suggested answers or completions. Select the one that BEST answers the question or completes the statement. *PRINT THE LETTER OF THE CORRECT ANSWER IN THE SPACE AT THE RIGHT.*

1. An employee under your supervision complains that he is assigned to work late more often than any of the other employees in the garage. You check the records and find that this isn't so. 1.____
You should

   A. advise this employee not to worry about what the other employees do but to see that he puts in a full day's work himself
   B. explain to this employee that you get the same complaint from all the other employees
   C. inform this employee that you have checked the records and the complaint is not justified
   D. not assign this employee to work late for a few days in order to keep him satisfied

2. A garage employee has reported late for work several times. 2.____
His supervisor should

   A. give this employee less desirable assignments
   B. overlook the lateness if the employee's work is otherwise exceptional
   C. recommend disciplinary action for habitual lateness
   D. talk the matter over with the employee before doing anything further

3. In choosing a man to be in charge in his absence, the supervisor should select first the employee who 3.____

   A. has ability to supervise others
   B. has been longest with the organization
   C. has the nicest appearance and manner
   D. is most skilled in his assigned duties

4. An employee under your supervision comes to you to complain about a decision you have made in assigning the men. He is excited and angry. You think what he is complaining about is not important, but it seems very important to him. 4.____
The BEST way for you to handle this is to

   A. let him talk until *he gets it off his chest* and then explain the reasons for your decision
   B. refuse to talk to him until he has cooled off
   C. show him at once how unimportant the matter is and how ridiculous his arguments are
   D. tell him to take it up with your superior if he disagrees with your decision

5. Suppose that a new employee has been appointed and assigned to your supervision. 5.____
When this man reports for work, it would be BEST for you to

A. ask him questions about different problems connected with a motor vehicle and see if he answers them correctly
B. check him carefully while he carries out some routine assignment that you give him
C. explain to him the general nature of the work he will be required to do
D. make a careful study of his previous work record before coming to the Department

6. The competent supervisor will be friendly with the employees under his supervision but will avoid close familiarity. 6.____
This statement is justified MAINLY because

A. a friendly attitude on the part of the supervisor toward the employee is likely to cause suspicion on the part of the employee
B. a supervisor can handle his employees better if he doesn't know their personal problems
C. close familiarity may interfere with the discipline needed for good supervisor-subordinate relationships
D. familiarity with the employees may be a sign of lack of ability on the part of the supervisor

7. An employee disagrees with the instructions that you, his supervisor, have given him for carrying out a certain assignment. 7.____
The BEST action for you to take is to tell this employee that

A. he can do what he wants but you will hold him responsible for failure
B. orders must be carried out or morale will fall apart
C. this job has been done in this way for many years with great success
D. you will be glad to listen to his objections and to his suggestions for improvement

8. As a supervisor, it is LEAST important for you to use a new employee's probationary period for the purpose of 8.____

A. carefully checking how he performs the work you assign him
B. determining whether he can perform the duties of his job efficiently
C. preparing him for promotion to a higher position
D. showing him how to carry out his assigned duties properly

9. Suppose you have just given an employee under your supervision instructions on how to carry out a certain assignment. 9.____
The BEST way to check that he has understood your instructions is to

A. ask him to repeat your instructions word for word
B. check the progress of his work the first chance you get
C. invite him to ask questions if he has any doubts
D. question him briefly about the main points of the assignment

10. Suppose you find it necessary to change a procedure that the men under your supervision have been following for a long time. 10.____
A good way to get their cooperation for this change would be to

A. bring them together to talk over the new procedure and explain the reasons for its adoption
B. explain to the men that if most of them still don't approve of the change after giving it a fair try, you will consider giving it up

C. give them a few weeks' notice of the proposed change in procedure
D. not enforce the new procedure strictly at the beginning

11. An order can be given by a supervisor in such a way as to make the employee want to obey it. 11.____
According to this statement, it is MOST reasonable to suppose that

A. a person will be glad to obey an order if he realizes that he must
B. if an order is given properly, it will be obeyed more willingly
C. it is easier to obey an order than to give one correctly
D. supervisors should inspire confidence by their actions as well as by their words

12. If one of the men you supervise disagrees with how you rate his work, the BEST way for you to handle this is to 12.____

A. advise him to appeal to your superior about it
B. decline to discuss the matter with him in order to keep discipline
C. explain why you rate him the way you do and talk it over with him
D. tell him that you are better qualified to rate his work than he is

13. A supervisor should be familiar with the experience and abilities of the employees under his supervision MAINLY because 13.____

A. each employee's work is highly important and requires a person of outstanding ability
B. it will help him to know which employees are best fitted for certain assignments
C. nearly all men have the same basic ability to do any job equally well
D. superior background shortly shows itself in superior work quality, regardless of assignment

14. The competent supervisor will try to develop respect rather than fear in his subordinates. 14.____
This statement is justified MAINLY because

A. fear is always present and, for best results, respect must be developed to offset it
B. it is generally easier to develop respect in the men than it is to develop fear
C. men who respect their supervisor are more likely to give more than the required minimum amount and quality of work
D. respect is based on the individual and fear is based on the organization as a whole

15. If one of the employees you supervise does outstanding work, you should 15.____

A. explain to him how his work can still be improved so that he will not become self-satisfied
B. mildly criticize the other men for not doing as good a job as this man
C. praise him for his work so that he will know it is appreciated
D. say nothing or he might become conceited

16. A supervisor can BEST help establish good morale among his employees if he 16.____

A. confides in them about his personal problems in order to encourage them to confide in him
B. encourages them to become friendly with him but discourages social engagements with them

C. points out to them the advantages of having a cooperative spirit in the department
D. sticks to the same rules that he expects them to follow

17. The one of the following situations which would seem to indicate poor scheduling of work by the supervisor in a garage is 17.____

A. everybody in the garage seeming to be very busy at the same time
B. re-assignment of a man to other work because of breakdown of a piece of equipment
C. two employees on vacation at the same time
D. two operators waiting to have their vehicles greased and the oil changed

Questions 18-20.

DIRECTIONS: Questions 18 through 20 are to be answered ONLY on the basis of the information given in the following paragraph.

The supervisor will gain the respect of the members of his staff and increase his influence over them by controlling his temper and avoiding criticizing anyone publicly. When a mistake is made, the good supervisor will talk it over with the employee quietly and privately. The supervisor will listen to the employee's story, suggest the better way of doing the job, and offer help so the mistake won't happen again. Before closing the discussion, the supervisor should try to find something good to say about other parts of the employee's work. Some praise and appreciation, along with instruction, is more likely to encourage an employee to improve in those areas where he is weakest.

18. A good title that would show the meaning of this entire paragraph would be 18.____

A. How to Correct Employee Errors
B. How to Praise Employees
C. Mistakes are Preventable
D. The Weak Employe

19. According to the above paragraph, the work of an employee who has made a mistake is more likely to improve if the supervisor 19.____

A. avoids criticizing him
B. gives him a chance to suggest a better way of doing the work
C. listens to the employee's excuses to see if he is right
D. praises good work at the same time he corrects the mistake

20. According to the above paragraph, when a supervisor needs to correct an employee's mistake, it is important that he 20.____

A. allow some time to go by after the mistake is made
B. do so when other employees are not present
C. show his influence with his tone of voice
D. tell other employees to avoid the same mistake

Questions 21-24.

DIRECTIONS: Questions 21 through 24 are to be answered ONLY on the basis of the information given in the following paragraph.

All automotive accidents, no matter how slight, are to be reported to the Safety Division by the employee involved on Accident Report Form S-23 in duplicate. When the accident is of such a nature that it requires the filling out of the State Motor Vehicle Report Form MV-104, this form is also prepared by the employee in duplicate and sent to the Safety Division for comparison with the Form S-23. The Safety Division forwards both copies of Form MV-104 to the Corporation Counsel, who sends one copy to the State Bureau of Motor Vehicles. When the information on the Form S-23 indicates that the employee may be at fault, an investigation is made by the Safety Division. If this investigation shows that the employee was at faulty the employee's dispatcher is asked to file a complaint on Form D-11. The foreman of mechanics prepares a damage report on Form D-8 and an estimate of the cost of repairs on Form D-9. The dispatcher's complaint, the damage report, the repair estimate, and the employee's previous accident record are sent to the Safety Division where they are studied together with the accident report. The Safety Division then recommends whether or not disciplinary action should be taken against the employee.

21. According to the above paragraph, the Safety Division should be notified whenever an automotive accident has occurred by means of 21.____

    A. Form S-23
    B. Forms S-23 and MV-104
    C. Forms S-23, MV-104, D-8, D-9, and D-11
    D. Forms S-23, MV-104, D-8, D-9, and D-11 and employee's accident report

22. According to the above paragraph, the forwarding of the Form MV-104 to the State Bureau of Motor Vehicles is done by the 22.____

    A. Corporation Counsel
    B. dispatcher
    C. employee involved in the accident
    D. Safety Division

23. According to the above paragraph, the Safety Division investigates an automotive accident if the 23.____

    A. accident is serious enough to be reported to the State Bureau of Motor Vehicles
    B. dispatcher files a complaint
    C. employee appears to have been at fault
    D. employee's previous accident report is poor

24. Of the forms mentioned in the above paragraph, the dispatcher is responsible for preparing the 24.____

    A. accident report form
    B. complaint form
    C. damage report
    D. estimate of cost of repairs

Questions 25-27.

DIRECTIONS: Questions 25 through 27 are to be answered ONLY on the basis of the information given in the following paragraph.

One of the major problems in the control of city motor equipment, and especially passenger equipment, is keeping the equipment working for the city and for the city alone for as many hours of the day as is practical. Even when most city employees try to get the most out of the cars, a poor system of control will result in wasted car hours. Some city employees have a legitimate use for a car all day long while others use a car only a small part of the day and then let it stand. As a rule, trucks are easier to control than passenger cars because they are usually assigned to a specific job where a foreman continually oversees them. Even though trucks are usually fully utilized, there are times when the normal work assignment cannot be carried out because of weather conditions or seasonal changes. At such times, a control system could plan to make the trucks available for other uses.

25. According to the above paragraph, a problem connected with controlling the use of city motor equipment is 25.____

    A. increasing the life span of the equipment
    B. keeping the equipment working all hours of the day
    C. preventing the over-use of the equipment to avoid breakdowns
    D. preventing the private use of the equipment

26. According to the above paragraph, a good control system for passenger equipment will MOST likely lead to 26.____

    A. better employees being assigned to operate the cars
    B. fewer city employees using city cars
    C. fewer wasted car hours for city cars
    D. insuring that city cars are used for legitimate purposes

27. According to the above paragraph, a control system for trucks is useful because 27.____

    A. a foreman usually supervises each job
    B. special conditions sometimes prevent the planned use of a truck
    C. trucks are easier to control than passenger cars
    D. trucks are usually assigned to specific jobs where they cannot be fully utilized

Questions 28-33.

DIRECTIONS: In the paragraph below, some of the underlined words have been purposely changed and spoil the meaning that the rest of the paragraph is meant to give. Read the paragraph carefully, then answer Questions 28 through 33.

The motor vehicle supervisor who is <u>responsible</u> for training drivers in the operation of <u>special</u> equipment cannot expect a man to carry out all of his duties <u>poorly</u> <u>immediately</u> after receiving instruction. The employee may be <u>overwhelmed</u> by all of the details he must master, <u>happy</u> because he is <u>associated</u> with new fellow workers, or fearful that he may not <u>succeed</u> on the job. It is the supervisor's <u>job</u> to make the <u>operator</u> feel at ease and <u>discourage</u> his self-confidence. The supervisor must also vary the speed of the <u>driving</u> according to the operator's <u>capacity</u> to <u>absorb</u> the instruction without undue <u>pressure</u> or confusion. All learners <u>progress</u> through <u>several</u> stages of <u>development</u> <u>unless</u> they become expert in their duties. As the operator's skills <u>increase</u>, he will require <u>more</u> instruction but the supervisor should be available to correct <u>mistakes</u> promptly to prevent wrong <u>habits</u> being formed.

28. Of the following words underlined in the above paragraph, the one that does NOT give the real meaning that the rest of the paragraph is meant to give is 28.____

A. responsible
B. special
C. happy
D. immediately

29. Of the following words underlined in the above paragraph, the one that does NOT give the real meaning that the rest of the paragraph is meant to give is 29.____

A. overwhelmed
B. happy
C. associated
D. succeed

30. Of the following words underlined in the above paragraph, the one that does NOT give the real meaning that the rest of the paragraph is meant to give is 30.____

A. job
B. operator
C. discourage
D. self-confidence

31. Of the following words underlined in the above paragraph, the one that does NOT give the real meaning that the rest of the paragraph is meant to give is 31.____

A. driving B. capacity C. absorb D. pressure

32. Of the following words underlined in the above paragraph, the one that does NOT give the real meaning that the rest of the paragraph is meant to give is 32.____

A. progress
B. several
C. development
D. unless

33. Of the following words underlined in the above paragraph, the one that does NOT give the real meaning that the rest of the paragraph is meant to give is 33.____

A. increase B. more C. mistakes D. habits

Questions 34-40.

DIRECTIONS: Each of Questions 34 through 40 consists of a word in capital letters followed by four suggested meanings of the word. Select the word or phrase which means MOST NEARLY the same as the word in capital letters.

34. ACCELERATE 34.____

A. adjust B. press C. quicken D. strip

35. ALIGN 35.____

A. bring into line
B. carry out
C. happen by chance
D. join together

36. CONTRACTION 36.____

A. agreement
B. denial
C. presentation
D. shrinkage

37. INTERVAL 37.____

A. ending
B. mixing together of
C. space of time
D. weaken

38. LUBRICATE 38.____

A. bend back
B. make slippery
C. rub out
D. soften

39. OBSOLETE 39.____

A. broken-down
B. hard to find
C. high-priced
D. out of date

40. RETARD 40.____

A. delay
B. flatten
C. rest
D. tally

KEY (CORRECT ANSWERS)

1. C	11. B	21. A	31. A
2. D	12. C	22. A	32. D
3. A	13. B	23. C	33. B
4. A	14. C	24. B	34. C
5. C	15. C	25. D	35. A
6. C	16. D	26. C	36. D
7. D	17. D	27. B	37. C
8. C	18. A	28. C	38. B
9. D	19. D	29. B	39. D
10. A	20. B	30. C	40. A

TEST 2

DIRECTIONS: Each question or incomplete statement is followed by several suggested answers or completions. Select the one that BEST answers the question or completes the statement. *PRINT THE LETTER OF THE CORRECT ANSWER IN THE SPACE AT THE RIGHT.*

Questions 1-3.

DIRECTIONS: Questions 1 through 3 consist of a word in capital letters followed by four suggested meanings of the word. Select the word or phrase which means MOST NEARLY the same as the word in capital letters.

1. SYNCHRONIZE 1.____

   A. draw out
   B. happen at the same time
   C. move at a steady rate
   D. turn smoothly

2. OSCILLATE 2.____

   A. attract
   B. echo
   C. roll
   D. swing

3. TERMINAL 3.____

   A. last
   B. moldy
   C. named
   D. spoken

4. In a certain garage, when the dispatcher issues gas and oil to a vehicle, he notes on his record the mileage reading of the vehicle. 4.____
   This is probably done MAINLY in order to

   A. check gas consumption against distance traveled
   B. compare age of vehicle with economy of operation
   C. decide when the vehicle should be scheduled for a grease job
   D. estimate future life expectancy of the vehicle

5. A supervisor of motor vehicle equipment was asked by the head of the bureau to investigate a certain procedure used in the garage and write a report with a recommendation whether the procedure should be changed. The supervisor, after he finished his investigation, made his report in which he said: *I recommend that you base your decision* to change the present procedure on whether or not the new procedure will improve operations. 5.____
   In this case, the supervisor carried out his assignment

   A. *poorly,* because he should have given his recommendation right at the beginning of the report
   B. *poorly,* because his investigation should have brought out whether the new procedure would improve operations
   C. *well,* because he left the final decision about changing the procedure up to the head of the bureau
   D. *well,* because he made an investigation and turned in a report as required

6. When a supervisor writes a report, it is LEAST important that 6.____

A. all paragraphs in the report be of the same length
B. a summary or list of the recommendations be given at the beginning of the report if the report is long
C. independent ideas be taken up in separate paragraphs of the report
D. the report give all the evidence on which the conclusions are based

7. The supervisor who makes a special point of using long words in preparing written reports is, in general, PROBABLY being 7.____

A. *unwise,* because a written report should be factual and accurate
B. *unwise,* because simplicity in a report is usually desirable
C. *wise,* because the written report will become a permanent record
D. *wise,* because with long words he can use the right emphasis in his report

8. The most thorough investigation is of no value if the report written by the person who made the investigation does not help his superior to decide what action to take. 8.____
According to this statement, it is LEAST correct to suppose that

A. an investigation is of no value unless it is thorough
B. a purpose of the report turned in after an investigation is to help supervisors decide what action to take
C. the report on an investigation is usually written by the person who made the investigation
D. the value of an investigation depends in part on the report turned in

9. Before you turn in a report you have written of an investigation that you made, you discover some additional information that you didn't know about before. 9.____
Whether or not you rewrite your report to include this additional information should depend MAINLY on the

A. amount of time left in which to submit the report
B. effect this information will have on the conclusions of the report
C. number of changes that you will have to make in your original report
D. possibility of turning in a supplementary report later

10. The advantage of using an *inspection check sheet* when making inspections of premises or equipment is that 10.____

A. fewer inspections are required
B. the inspection becomes easy and can be done by a subordinate
C. there is less chance of forgetting some important point of the inspection
D. there is less paper work

11. Of the following methods for keeping supplies and records of supplies, the one that will MOST quickly tell you at any time how many pieces of any item are on hand in the supply room is 11.____

A. keeping a minimum number of each item on hand
B. recording each item when it is added to or removed from stock
C. stocking the same number of pieces of each item and reordering weekly to keep the count even
D. taking a daily count

12. When a supervisor submits a report on a motor vehicle accident, it is LEAST important for him to include in his report the 12.____

    A. addresses of the witnesses to the accident
    B. number of the police precinct where the accident happened
    C. probable cause of the accident
    D. time of the accident

13. The MAIN reason a supervisor in charge of motor vehicle equipment or personnel should make sure that his men obey the safety rules is that 13.____

    A. accident prevention is a new program and should be tried out
    B. every accident can be prevented
    C. other safety measures are not needed where safety rules are obeyed
    D. safety rules are based on proven methods of accident prevention

14. When he investigates an accident in which a city vehicle was involved, the MAIN object of the supervisor should be to 14.____

    A. complete the investigation as fast as possible
    B. determine if the city operator's record is so bad that he should be fired
    C. get all the facts to establish the cause of the accident
    D. try to establish that the other driver was at least equally to blame

15. If witnesses to an automobile accident are interviewed separately, they are more likely to give different versions of the circumstances of the accident than if they are interviewed together.
    According to this statement, it is MOST probable that 15.____

    A. a truer picture of the circumstances of an accident can be gotten by interviewing the witnesses together rather than separately
    B. a witness's impression of what he saw is influenced by the statement of the other witnesses as to what they saw
    C. people who see an accident as a group will agree about the details of the accident more than people who are not together when they see the accident
    D. witnesses are less likely to tell the truth when interviewed privately than when interviewed as a group

16. A thorough investigation should always be made of an accident in which a city vehicle is involved.
    The MAIN value of such an investigation is to 16.____

    A. discover any factors that contributed to the accident which may be corrected
    B. keep compensation claims down
    C. provide good records from which statistics can be developed
    D. show the operators that accidents are taken seriously, no matter how small

17. An accident has been described as *an unplanned event caused by an unsafe act or condition.*
    An example of an unsafe act, rather than of an unsafe condition, in a garage is 17.____

    A. blocked fire exits
    B. defective tools or equipment
    C. horseplay or teasing
    D. oil and grease on floors

18. Of the following rules, the one that is LEAST directly concerned with the prevention of accidents is: 18.____

A. Check brake fluid before leaving garage
B. Do not use garage equipment if safety devices do not work
C. No smoking in garage
D. Reports of time lost due to accident must be submitted in 5 days

19. Which of the following entries on a Department Accident Report Form is MAINLY for the purpose of showing what is being done so that this type of accident will not happen again? 19.____

A. Describe accident, including vehicle or vehicles involved
B. What are you doing to prevent similar accidents?
C. Why did the unsafe condition exist?
D. Why was the unsafe act committed?

20. With respect to motor vehicle accidents, it is necessary to report in duplicate to the Bureau of Motor Vehicles on its printed forms 20.____

A. all accidents
B. only those accidents in which someone is killed or injured
C. only those accidents in which someone is killed or injured or there is property damage of more than $50
D. only those accidents in which someone is killed or injured or there is property damage of more than $100

21. A section of a garage used for parking vehicle measures 162 1/2' x 25 3/4'. 21.____
If each vehicle to be parked in this section requires, on the average, 84 sq.ft. of parking space, the MAXIMUM number of vehicles that can be parked in this section is CLOSEST to

A. 50 B. 45 C. 40 D. 35

22. Each of the 23 vehicles in a garage uses an average of 114 gallons of gas every 4 weeks. 22.____
If the motor vehicle dispatcher is required to re-order gas when the gas tank in the garage shows no more than a one week supply, he MUST re-order when the gas tank shows ______ gallons.

A. 655 B. 705 C. 830 D. 960

23. An employee's annual salary is $45,800. His total and annual deductions are 22% for withholding tax, 8 1/2% for pension and social security, and $1,820 for health insurance. 23.____
The take-home pay that this employee would get on the check he receives every other week is MOST NEARLY

A. $577.10 B. $845.00 C. $1,154.20 D. $1,220.40

24. A vehicle which averages 14 1/2 miles to a gallon of gas uses a quart of oil for every 21 1/2 gallons of gas. 24.____
If the vehicle traveled 19,952 miles in a year, its oil consumption for the year would be ______ quarts.

A. 52 B. 56 C. 60 D. 64

25. Thirteen percent of all the vehicles in a certain garage are trucks. 25.____
If there are 26 trucks, then the number of vehicles of other types in this garage is

A. 174 B. 200 C. 260 D. 338

26. Of 12 employees in a garage, four earn $3,500 a year, two earn $3,150 a year, one earns $4,550 a year, and the rest each earn $3,800 a year. 26.____
The average yearly salary of these employees is CLOSEST to

A. $3,550 B. $3,650 C. $3,750 D. $3,850

27. A garage bin used for storing supplies and parts measures 1 yard x 2 yards x 7 feet. 27.____
The cubic volume of this bin is

A. 5 1/3 cubic yards
B. 16 cubic feet
C. 63 cubic feet
D. 126 cubic feet

28. A garage has a gas tank with a capacity of 1,300 gallons. If there are only 520 gallons of gas in the tank, then the tank is _______ full. 28.____

A. 40% B. 33 1/3% C. 25% D. 16 3/4%

29. Of a specially selected group of vehicles, 1/5 are 6 months old, 2/5 are 12 months old, and 2/5 are 15 months old. 29.____
The average age of this group of vehicles is _______ months.

A. 9 B. 10 C. 11 D. 12

30. A suggestion has been made that every vehicle have its gas tank filled and oil and water checked when it returns to the garage at the end of the day. 30.____
This suggestion is

A. *good,* mainly because the gas pump can be kept locked the rest of the day
B. *good,* mainly because vehicles will be ready to go out promptly the next day
C. *poor,* mainly because it would take too long to fill each vehicle
D. *poor,* mainly because not every vehicle will need gas, oil, and water

31. Brakes do not generally have to be adjusted until the clearance between the bottom of the brake pedal and the floorboard goes below _______ inch(es). 31.____

A. 2-2 1/2 B. 1 1/2-2 C. 1-1 1/2 D. 1/2-1

32. *Play* in the steering wheel is generally NOT considered to be excessive until it reaches about _______ inch(es). 32.____

A. 1/2 B. 1 C. 1 1/2 D. 2

33. If the oil pressure gauge in a sedan reads unduly high even after the engine is warmed up, the MOST probable reason is 33.____

A. a low oil level in the crankcase
B. an internal leak in the oil system
C. an obstruction in the oil line
D. too light an oil being used

34. In order to keep tire pressure at the level recommended by the manufacturer, the air pressure in the tires should be 34.____

A. checked at the end of the day's driving
B. checked in the morning, before the vehicle is driven
C. lower in summer than in winter
D. reduced before a long trip to leave room for expansion

35. When inspecting one of your vehicles, you notice excessive wear on the center of the tread of both front tires. 35.____
This unusual wear is MOST likely caused by

A. excessive toe-in of the front wheels
B. over-inflation of the front tires
C. too much camber of the front wheels
D. under-inflation of the front tires

36. The level of the fluid in the battery should be _______ the top of the plates. 36.____

A. barely covering
B. exactly even with
C. well below
D. well over

37. A heavy layer of oil on the water in the radiator would MOST probably indicate a 37.____

A. cracked block
B. dirty air cleaner
C. loose hose connection
D. water pump leak

38. If a five gallon can of gasoline is spilled on the garage floor, the BEST action to take is to 38.____

A. let the gasoline evaporate
B. pour sand over the puddle of gasoline
C. squirt a foam-producing fire extinguisher on the puddle
D. use a hose to flush the gasoline away

39. Greasy rags and waste in a garage should be 39.____

A. hung up on a line to air out
B. put in boxes that will be emptied daily
C. put in covered metal cans or barrels
D. put in wire baskets outside the garage

40. Adjusting the carburetor to give a mixture that is richer in fuel is 40.____

A. *good* practice in cold weather as it improves engine operation
B. *good* practice in very hot weather as it prevents stalling
C. *poor* practice as it increases the chance of vapor lock
D. *poor* practice in stop-and-go city driving as it greatly increases gas consumption

KEY (CORRECT ANSWERS)

1.	B	11.	B	21.	A	31.	C
2.	D	12.	B	22.	A	32.	D
3.	A	13.	D	23.	C	33.	C
4.	A	14.	C	24.	D	34.	B
5.	B	15.	B	25.	A	35.	B
6.	A	16.	A	26.	B	36.	D
7.	B	17.	C	27.	D	37.	A
8.	A	18.	D	28.	A	38.	D
9.	B	19.	B	29.	D	39.	C
10.	C	20.	D	30.	B	40.	A

TEST 3

DIRECTIONS: Each question or incomplete statement is followed by several suggested answers or completions. Select the one that BEST answers the question or completes the statement. *PRINT THE LETTER OF THE CORRECT ANSWER IN THE SPACE AT THE RIGHT.*

Questions 1-10.

DIRECTIONS: Questions 1 through 10 are based on the information given in the map on page 2.

1. On pay day, you assign an operator to deliver paychecks by car to the four work crews assigned to street jobs in the area. He starts from the garage and is to return there when finished. 1.____
   The order of delivery that would take the operator over the shortest allowable route would be crew

   A. 1, 2, 3, 4
   B. 2, 1, 4, 3
   C. 3, 2, 1, 4
   D. 4, 3, 2, 1

2. Work crew 4 will be finished with its job at 1 P.M. and has to be moved to a new work location at Fir Ave. and 5th St. Work crew 3 will be finished with its job at the same time and has to be moved to begin work on a new job at 6th St. and Elm Ave. The operator assigned to the truck is to start from and return to the garage. 2.____
   In order to get each of these crews to their new locations as soon as possible, the dispatcher should instruct the operator assigned to pick up crew

   A. 3 and drop them at their new location; then pick up crew 4 and drop them at their new location
   B. 4 and drop them at their new location; pick up crew 3 and drop them at their new location
   C. 3; pick up crew 4; drop off crew 3; drop off crew 4
   D. 4; pick up crew 3; drop off crew 3; drop off crew 4

3. The shortest allowable route for driving from the repair shop to the garage is 2nd Street and 3.____

   A. Fir Ave.
   B. Gladiola Ave.
   C. Gladiola Ave., 3rd St., Fir Ave.
   D. Holly Ave., 1st St., Gladiola Ave.

4. You have requests for the following pick-ups and deliveries: a record player and loudspeaker to be moved from the playground to the skating rink, a case of pictures to be taken from the museum to the high school, and a ticket box to be moved from the stadium to the skating rink. 4.____
   Using the shortest allowable route from the garage and back, the order in which these pick-ups and deliveries should be made with the LEAST number of stops is

   A. museum, high school, playground, skating rink, stadium
   B. museum, playground, high school, stadium, skating rink
   C. playground, skating rink, museum, high school, stadium
   D. stadium, skating rink, museum, high school, playground

A ◯ indicates a street work crew.

A ✕ indicates a an entrance.

Arrows on streets indicate one-way and two-way streets.
No U turns are permitted.

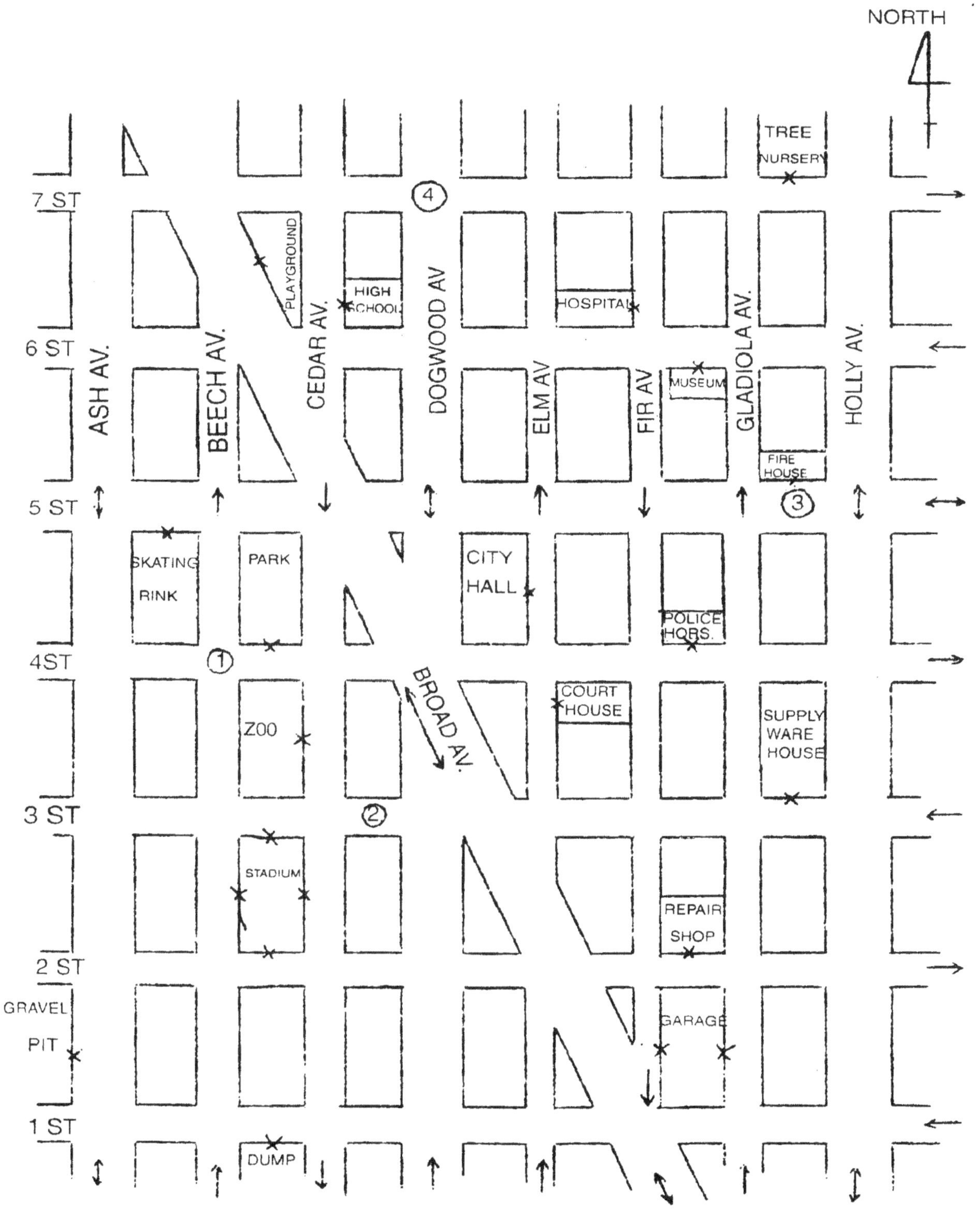

5. To help a newly assigned motor vehicle operator learn this area, you might ask him to study the direction of traffic patterns on the map.
It would be MOST helpful if you pointed out to him that two-way traffic is permitted on 5.____

A. all but one of the numbered streets
B. all but three of the named avenues
C. only one of the numbered streets
D. only three of the named avenues

6. In routing motor equipment to the northwestern part of the mapped area, the dispatcher would be wise to use Broad Avenue MAINLY because it is 6.____

A. a two-way street
B. a wide street
C. near the garage
D. the most direct route

7. A disadvantage of the construction and location of the repair shop, according to the map, is that 7.____

A. it has only one entrance on 2nd St.
B. it is located too close to the garage as equipment breakdowns would happen in the field
C. motor equipment leaving the garage must go around the block to enter the shop
D. the shop is too small in comparison to the size of the garage

8. Two factors about the construction and location of the garage that are of special advantage to the dispatcher are that it 8.____

A. has two entrances and is near the repair shop
B. has two entrances and one-way streets on all sides
C. is near the repair shop and occupies a whole block
D. occupies a whole block and has one-way streets on all sides

9. When dispatching equipment from the garage to the hospital, the dispatcher should use the entrance on 9.____

A. either Gladiola Ave. or Fir Ave.
B. Fir Ave.
C. Gladiola Ave.
D. 2nd St.

10. You have requests to pick up some small trees at the tree nursery to be delivered to the park, to pick up gravel at the gravel pit and deliver the load to the zoo, to take some broken benches from the park to the repair shop, to pick up supplies at the warehouse for delivery to City Hall and the court house.
The order in which a truck should do these jobs, starting from the garage and using the shortest allowable route is 10.____

A. gravel pit, zoo; park, repair shop; warehouse, court house, City Hall; tree nursery, park, garage
B. gravel pit, zoo; warehouse, court house, City Hall; tree nursery, park; park, repair shop; repair shop, garage
C. tree nursery, park; park, repair shop; zoo, gravel pit; warehouse, court house, City Hall, garage
D. warehouse, court house, City Hall; tree nursery, park; park, repair shop; gravel pit, zoo; zoo, garage

Questions 11-20.

DIRECTIONS: Answer Questions 11 through 20 ONLY on the basis of the information given below in the two charts and the Rules of the Department. You are to assume that you are the dispatcher in the garage where these charts are kept and where they are used in making daily assignments of operators and vehicles.

SECOND AVE. GARAGE MOTOR VEHICLE OPERATOR CONTROL SHEET Date: May 25, 19 __				SECOND AVE. GARAGE MOTOR VEHICLE OPERATOR CONTROL SHEET Date: May 25, 19 __			
Name of Operator	Cleared on	Hours of Overtime Credit as of May 25	On Vaca-tion	Vehicle Number and Type	In Re-pair Shop as of May 25	Date Due in Shop for Pre-ventive Mainten-ance In-spection	Date Last In Repair
Allen	P T	74		20-P		7/13	3/2
Boyd	P W	31	5/18-30	21-P		6/15	2/16
Cohen	P T	129		22-T		5/26	1/19
Diggs	P	15		23-P		6/1	5/8
Egan	P T	92	6/1-13	24-P		6/8	2/2
First	P T W	49		25-P		7/6	2/24
Gordon	P	57		26-W		6/1	1/21
Hanson	P T	143	6/15-27	27-T		7/20	4/6
				28-T	X	7/27	3/16
				29-P	X	5/18	1/12

Symbols: P - Passenger Car
T - Truck
W - Wrecker

Symbols: P - Passenger Car
T - Truck
W - Wrecker

RULES OF THE DEPARTMENT

1. A motor vehicle operator may be assigned to drive only those types of vehicles on which he has been cleared. No one but a motor vehicle operator may be assigned to drive a Department vehicle.

2. Private cars may not be used for Department business.

3. The motor vehicle dispatcher shall keep a daily record of overtime credits of all operators under his supervision to be sure that no operator acquires more than 150 hours of overtime credit. An assignment which involves overtime should be given, wherever possible, to the operator with the least overtime credit.

4. A vehicle due for preventive maintenance must be sent to the repair shop on the date it is due for preventive maintenance, except when a vehicle has been in the repair shop during the previous month.

5. All available vehicles are to be assigned to jobs as requested, with none held in reserve.

11. An official who is requesting a truck and operator for the three days beginning May 26th indicates to you that some overtime may be necessary for the operator, but he cannot predict how many hours of overtime will be needed. Under these circumstances, the MOST logical man for you to choose for this assignment would be operator 11.____

A. Allen B. Boyd C. Diggs D. First

12. The vehicle which does NOT have to be sent to the shop for preventive maintenance on the date it is due is vehicle number 12.____

A. 23 B. 25 C. 27 D. 29

13. As dispatcher, you receive a request on May 25th for a truck and motor vehicle operator for a job that will take three days, from May 26th through May 28th. 13.____
The vehicle that it would be BEST for you to choose on May 25th for this assignment is vehicle number

A. 28 B. 27 C. 22 D. 20

14. On May 25th, right after all the vehicles have left the garage on daily assignment, you receive a call from your Commissioner's secretary. She tells you that an emergency has come up and asks you for a car to be ready in fifteen minutes to take a messenger with important papers to be delivered to the Commissioner who is waiting for the papers at a court in another borough. 14.____
Of the following, the BEST thing for you to do, after explaining to the secretary that you have no cars available, is to

A. advise her she should give you advance notice the next time so that you can reserve a car for the messenger
B. offer to drive the messenger yourself in your private car
C. promise to get a car from another department
D. suggest that the messenger use public transportation

15. To give you more leeway in assigning your operators to the available equipment, it would be MOST practical for you to 15.____

A. ask your supervisor to assign two additional motor vehicle operators to the garage
B. have additional operators cleared on the wrecker
C. suggest to your supervisor that rule 3 be abolished
D. suggest to your supervisor that rule 1 be abolished

16. Other things being equal, the operator who should probably be of MOST value to you, as the dispatcher, is 16.____

A. Cohen B. Diggs C. First D. Hanson

17. The factor which indicates MOST strongly that there may not be enough operators assigned to this garage is the 17.____

A. amount of overtime accumulated
B. excess of number of vehicles over number of operators
C. incomplete vacation schedule
D. number of operators cleared on trucks

18. When dispatching men and equipment in the morning, it would be BEST for you to first dispatch men who 18.____

A. are cleared on 1 vehicle
B. are cleared on 2 vehicles
C. are cleared on 3 vehicles
D. have already had their vacations

19. The second week in June, you receive a call for an operator and wrecker. It is better to dispatch Boyd rather than First because 19.____

A. he has already had his vacation
B. he has less overtime
C. he is not cleared on trucks
D. unless there are special reasons, you might as well assign the men in alphabetical order for easier record keeping

20. You have requests for 6 passenger cars and 2 trucks for jobs on May 25th. All of these jobs will probably take the full day but none will require any overtime. How many of these requests for May 25th would you have to refuse? 20.____

A. None
B. One
C. Two
D. More than two

KEY (CORRECT ANSWERS)

1.	B	11.	D
2.	A	12.	A
3.	D	13.	B
4.	B	14.	D
5.	C	15.	B
6.	D	16.	C
7.	C	17.	A
8.	A	18.	A
9.	C	19.	C
10.	B	20.	B

TEST 4

DIRECTIONS: Each question or incomplete statement is followed by several suggested answers or completions. Select the one that BEST answers the question or completes the statement. *PRINT THE LETTER OF THE CORRECT ANSWER IN THE SPACE AT THE RIGHT.*

1. In a program of switching tires on a vehicle at regular intervals to give longer tire life, the BEST system to follow is 1.____

A. 
B. 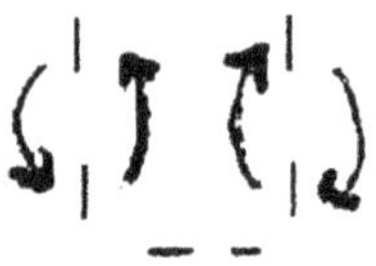
C. 
D. 

2. If an engine misfires when it is operated at low speed, the order in which the items below should be inspected, tested, and adjusted is 2.____

   A. breaker contact points, distributor cap and rotor, high voltage wires, spark plugs
   B. distributor cap and rotor, breaker contact points, spark plugs, high voltage wires
   C. high voltage wires, spark plugs, breaker contact points, distributor can and rotor
   D. spark plugs, high voltage wires, distributor cap and rotor, breaker contact points

3. An operator complains that the headlights on his vehicle flare up and then dim as the speed of the vehicle changes. 3.____
The MOST probable cause is

   A. a burned out fuse or defective circuit breaker
   B. a defective dimmer switch
   C. a loose connection in the headlight wiring
   D. weak bulbs

4. A can of motor oil is marked *S.A.E. 20-20W.* 4.____
This indicates that

   A. a mistake was made, and the oil should not be used
   B. chemicals have been added to winterize the oil
   C. the oil may be used both in medium temperatures and in winter weather
   D. the oil should be used when the temperature is between 20 degrees below and 20 degrees above zero

5. A specific gravity reading of 1280 at 80° F means that a battery is 5.____

   A. fully discharged
   B. nearing a discharged condition
   C. about half charged
   D. fully charged

6. If a generator constantly charges at a high rate, it is MOST probably due to a(n) 6.____

   A. defective regulator
   B. dirty commutator
   C. too tight fan belt adjustment
   D. overcharged battery

7. In the servicing of spark plugs, it is IMPORTANT to 7.____

A. bend the center electrode rather than the side electrode when adjusting the spark plug gap
B. clean the spark plug recess in the cylinder head with a brush or compressed air after a spark plug has been removed
C. make sure that each spark plug has only one gasket
D. use an adjustable wrench to tighten a spark plug in its hole

8. If air gets into the lines of a hydraulic brake system, the MOST likely result will be 8.____

A. a spongy pedal
B. grabbing brakes
C. locked brakes
D. a hard pedal

9. In hooking test ammeters and voltmeters into a circuit, the ammeter 9.____

A. should be connected in parallel and the voltmeter in series
B. should be connected in series and the voltmeter in parallel
C. and voltmeter should be connected in parallel
D. and voltmeter should be connected in series

10. When brakes are correctly adjusted but one wheel takes hold before the others, it is MOST likely that the 10.____

A. cup on the wheel cylinder has swelled
B. relief port on the master cylinder isn't working
C. push rod adjustment is faulty
D. brake fluid has leaked into the lining

11. Racing an automobile engine on cold mornings to warm it up is 11.____

A. *bad* practice, because there is poor lubrication of moving parts
B. *good* practice, because the oil will reach moving parts faster
C. *bad* practice, because it will form sludge in the engine
D. *good* practice, because it will allow liquid gasoline to reach the crankcase

12. Using anti-freeze solution for more than a single season is 12.____

A. *bad* practice, because it will cause excessive rust
B. *good* practice, because it will be economical
C. *bad* practice, because it will raise the boiling point
D. *good* practice, because it will not clog the cooling system

13. The one of the following which is NOT usually a purpose of a preventive maintenance program for a fleet of automotive vehicles is 13.____

A. a greater margin of safety in the operation of the vehicles
B. easier and more comfortable driving
C. improved mechanical ability of vehicle operators
D. increased economy in vehicle operations

14. The one of the following which will NOT help improve gasoline mileage is 14.____

A. driving at high speeds
B. even acceleration
C. keeping tires at recommended pressure
D. using light oil in winter

15. An abnormally cool brake drum on one wheel after the vehicle has been in operation would MOST probably indicate a(n) 15.____

A. dragging shoe
B. improperly adjusted brake drum
C. non-functioning brake
D. underlubricated bearing

16. The pitman arm is part of the 16.____

A. brake shoe assembly
B. driving axle
C. fan belt assembly
D. steering mechanism

17. When he returns to the garage at the end of his shift, a motor vehicle operator complains to you that the engine *skips* on the car he is driving. 17.____
When you prepare your requisition for a check-up of this vehicle, it is LEAST important for you to ask for a check of the

A. battery
B. carburetor
C. condenser
D. fuel line

18. In a garage where a vehicle preventive maintenance program is in operation, the one of the following which it is MOST important to do right away without waiting for next checkup is 18.____

A. adjusting brakes that pull unevenly
B. changing oil and lubrication to summer or winter grades
C. checking spark plugs
D. replacing an oil-soaked water hose

19. To test whether every cylinder has good compression, the instrument that should be used is a 19.____

A. vacuum gauge
B. gas analyzer
C. creeper
D. vent ball

20. It is generally recommended that the radiator of a passenger vehicle be flushed out 20.____

A. every 1,000 miles
B. every fall and spring
C. every 2,000 miles
D. once a year

KEY (CORRECT ANSWERS)

1. A
2. D
3. C
4. C
5. D
6. A
7. C
8. A
9. B
10. D
11. A
12. A
13. C
14. A
15. C
16. D
17. A
18. A
19. A
20. B

WORK SCHEDULING
EXAMINATION SECTION
TEST 1

DIRECTIONS: Each question or incomplete statement is followed by several suggested answers or completions. Select the one that BEST answers the question or completes the statement. *PRINT THE LETTER OF THE CORRECT ANSWER IN THE SPACE AT THE RIGHT.*

Questions 1-8.

DIRECTIONS: Questions 1 through 8 are to be answered on the basis of the following information.

Assume that you are the supervisor of a unit that works seven days a week. You need to determine the work and vacation schedules of the employees you supervise for the month of July.

<u>THE EMPLOYEES</u>

Alan W.	9 years seniority	computer operator
Jane B.	4 1/2 years seniority	typist
Alex H.	5 years seniority	security staff
Tony E.	4 years seniority	security staff
Andre T.	4 2/3 years seniority	typist
Mary W.	11 years seniority	security staff
Andy R.	13 years seniority	computer operator
Rhonda L.	2 years seniority	computer operator
Ethel R.	15 years seniority	typist
Roger G.	3 years seniority	security staff

<u>THE VACATION PREFERENCES OF THE EMPLOYEES</u>:

	1st vacation day	1ast vacation day
Alan W.	7/1	7/19
Jane B.	7/15	7/29
Alex H.	7/8	7/22
Tony E.	7/22	7/30
Andre T.	7/1	7/14
Mary W.	7/1	7/22
Andy R.	7/15	7/30
Rhonda L.	7/20	7/31
Ethel R.	7/1	7/27
Roger G.	7/21	7/31

<u>IMPORTANT REGULATIONS REGARDING VACATION LEAVE</u>

Employees with seniority have first choice for their preferred vacation dates. Seniority should be calculated separately for each of the three occupational groups.

There must be two security employees on duty each working day in July. This overrides any other considerations.

There must be one typist on duty each working day in July. This overrides any other considerations.

Employees with least seniority, when denied their first choice of vacation dates, should automatically be scheduled ahead for vacation on the very next date closest to the dates they had originally preferred and the length of the vacation extended the appropriate number of days. Example: A vacation originally requested for 7/13, but changed because of seniority, would be moved AHEAD to a date after 7/13 (to 7/16, for example).

You may want to use the calendar below to help you organize this information.

JULY

1	2	3	4	5	6	7
8	9	10	11	12	13	14
15	16	17	18	19	20	21
22	23	24	25	26	27	28
29	30	31				

1. The number of employees on vacation on July 16 should be 1.____
   A. four B. five C. six D. seven

2. The number of employees on vacation on July 22 should be 2.____
   A. five B. six C. seven D. eight

3. How many typists will be working on July 15? 3.____
   A. One B. Two C. Three D. None

4. How many workers will be on vacation on July 31? 4.____
   A. Two B. Three C. Four D. Five

5. Which of the following is TRUE of the employees in the unit? 5.____
   I. Andy R., Jane B., Tony E., and Mary W. will be on vacation on 7/22.
   II. Ethel R., Andre T., Mary W., and Alex H. will be on vacation on 7/8.

III. Rhonda L., Tony E., and Roger G. will be on vacation on 7/31, 5.____
IV. Andy R., Jane B., and Ethel R. will be on vacation on 7/28.

THE CORRECT ANSWER IS:

A. I, II, III
B. I, II
C. II, III
D. II

6. How many typists will be working on July 28? 6.____

A. One B. Two C. Three D. Four

7. How many computer operators will be working on July 23? 7.____

A. One B. Two C. Three D. Four

8. Roger G. will begin his vacation on July 8.____

A. 21 B. 22 C. 23 D. 24

Questions 9-15.

DIRECTIONS: Questions 9 through 15 are to be answered on the basis of the following information.

Assume that you are the supervisor of a unit that works seven days a week. You need to determine the work and vacation schedules of the employees you supervise for the month of August.

THE EMPLOYEES

	Years Seniority	Position
Robert L.	7	Security staff
Ann N.	71/2	Computer operator
Thomas B.	9	Typist
Phyllis P.	11	Computer operator
Mike D.	3	Security staff
Jane R.	2	Security staff
Alan R.	8	Computer operator
Susan T.	10	Typist
George W.	6	Computer operator
Barbara L.	4	Typist
Jack B.	13	Security staff
Grace N.	12	Typist

THE VACATION PREFERENCES OF THE EMPLOYEES

	1st vacation day	last vacation day
Robert L.	8/3	8/18
Ann N.	8/17	8/28
Thomas B.	8/19	8/28
Phyllis P.	8/5	8/20
Mike D.	8/14	8/21
Jane R.	8/20	8/27
Alan R.	8/12	8/26
Susan T.	8/5	8/26
George W.	8/3	8/14
Barbara L.	8/7	8/21
Jack B.	8/10	8/18
Grace N.	8/4	8/25

IMPORTANT REGULATIONS REGARDING VACATION LEAVE.

Employees with seniority have first choice for their preferred vacation dates. Seniority should be calculated separately for each of the three occupational groups.

There must be two security employees on duty each working day in August. This overrides any other considerations.

There must be two typists on duty from 8/11 to 8/18. This overrides any other considerations.

There must be two computer operators on duty each working day in August. This overrides any other considerations.

Employees with least seniority, when denied their first choice of vacation dates, should automatically be scheduled ahead for their vacation on the very next date closest to the date they originally preferred, and the length of the vacation extended the appropriate number of days. Example: A vacation originally requested for 8/18, but changed because of seniority, would be moved AHEAD to a date after 8/18 (to 8/21, for example).

You may wish to use the calendar on the next page to help you organize this information.

AUGUST

1	2	3	4	5	6	7
8	9	10	11	12	13	14
15	16	17	18	19	20	21
22	23	24	25	26	27	28
29	30	31				

9. How many workers will be on vacation on August 21? 9._____

   A. Five B. Six C. Seven D. Eight

10. How many workers will be working on August 28? 10._____

   A. Six B. Seven C. Eight D. Nine

11. Of the following, who will NOT work on August 27? 11.____

A. Alan R. B. George W. C. Mike D. D. Susan T.

12. Of the following, who will work on August 19? 12.____

A. Thomas B. B. Barbara L.
C. Ann N. D. Mike D.

13. How many typists will be on vacation on August 19? 13.____

A. One B. Two C. Three D. Four

14. How many workers will be on vacation on August 17? 14.____

A. Five B. Six C. Eight D. Nine

15. How many workers will work on August 11? 15.____

A. Seven B. Eight C. Five D. Six

KEY (CORRECT ANSWERS)

1.	C	6.	B	11.	B
2.	B	7.	A	12.	C
3.	A	8.	C	13.	D
4.	B	9.	D	14.	B
5.	C	10.	C	15.	A

RECORD KEEPING

EXAMINATION SECTION

TEST 1

DIRECTIONS: Each question or incomplete statement is followed by several suggested answers or completions. Select the one that BEST answers the question or completes the statement. *PRINT THE LETTER OF THE CORRECT ANSWER IN THE SPACE AT THE RIGHT.*

Questions 1-15.

DIRECTIONS: Questions 1 through 15 are to be answered on the basis of the following list of company names below. Arrange a file alphabetically, word-by-word, disregarding punctuation, conjunctions, and apostrophes. Then answer the questions.

A Bee C Reading Materials
ABCO Parts
A Better Course for Test Preparation
AAA Auto Parts Co.
A-Z Auto Parts, Inc.
Aabar Books
Abbey, Joanne
Boman-Sylvan Law Firm
BMW Autowerks
C Q Service Company
Chappell-Murray, Inc.
E&E Life Insurance
Emcrisco
Gigi Arts
Gordon, Jon & Associates
SOS Plumbing
Schmidt, J.B. Co.

1. Which of these files should appear FIRST? 1.____
   A. ABCO Parts
   B. A Bee C Reading Materials
   C. A Better Course for Test Preparation
   D. AAA Auto Parts Co.

2. Which of these files should appear SECOND? 2.____
   A. A-Z Auto Parts, Inc.
   B. A Bee C Reading Materials
   C. A Better Course for Test Preparation
   D. AAA Auto Parts Co.

3. Which of these files should appear THIRD? 3.____
   A. ABCO Parts
   B. A Bee C Reading Materials
   C. Aabar Books
   D. AAA Auto Parts Co.

4. Which of these files should appear FOURTH? 4.____
   A. Aabar Books
   B. ABCO Parts
   C. Abbey, Joanne
   D. AAA Auto Parts Co.

5. Which of these files should appear LAST? 5.____
   A. Gordon, Jon & Associates
   B. Gigi Arts
   C. Schmidt, J.B. Co.
   D. SOS Plumbing

6. Which of these files should appear between A-Z Auto Parts, Inc. and Abbey, Joanne? 6.____
   A. A Bee C Reading Materials
   B. AAA Auto Parts Co.
   C. ABCO Parts
   D. A Better Course for Test Preparation

7. Which of these files should appear between ABCO Parts and Aabar Books? 7.____
   A. A Bee C Reading Materials
   B. Abbey, Joanne
   C. Aabar Books
   D. A-Z Auto Parts

8. Which of these files should appear between Abbey, Joanne and Boman-Sylvan Law Firm? 8.____
   A. A Better Course for Test Preparation
   B. BMW Autowerks
   C. Chappell-Murray, Inc.
   D. Aabar Books

9. Which of these files should appear between Abbey, Joanne and C Q Service? 9.____
   A. A-Z Auto Parts, Inc.
   B. BMW Autowerks
   C. Choices A and B
   D. Chappell-Murray, Inc.

10. Which of these files should appear between C Q Service Company and Emcrisco? 10.____
   A. Chappell-Murray, Inc.
   B. E&E Life Insurance
   C. Gigi Arts
   D. Choices A and B

11. Which of these files should NOT appear between C Q Service Company and E&E Life Insurance? 11.____
   A. Gordon, Jon & Associates
   B. Emcrisco
   C. Gigi Arts
   D. All of the above

12. Which of these files should appear between Chappell-Murray, Inc. and Gigi Arts? 12.____
    A. C Q Service Inc., E&E Life Insurance, and Emcrisco
    B. Emcrisco, E&E Life Insurance, and Gordon, Jon & Associates
    C. E&E Life Insurance, and Emcrisco
    D. Emcrisco and Gordon, Jon & Associates

13. Which of these files should appear between Gordon, Jon & Associates and SOS Plumbing? 13.____
    A. Gigi Arts
    B. Schmidt,J.B. Co.
    C. Choices A and B
    D. None of the above

14. Each of the choices lists the four files in their proper alphabetical order EXCEPT 14.____
    A. E&E Life Insurance; Gigi Arts; Gordon, Jon & Associates; SOS Plumbing
    B. E&E Life Insurance; Emcrisco; Gigi Arts; SOS Plumbing
    C. Emcrisco; Gordon, Jon & Associates; SOS Plumbing; Schmidt, J.B. Co.
    D. Emcrisco; Gigi Arts; Gordon, Jon & Associates; SOS Plumbing

15. Which of the choices lists the four files in their proper alphabetical order? 15.____
    A. Gigi Arts; Gordon, Jon & Associates; SOS Plumbing; Schmidt, J.B. Co.
    B. Gordon, Jon & Associates; Gigi Arts; Schmidt, J.B. Co.; SOS Plumbing
    C. Gordon, Jon & Associates; Gigi Arts; SOS Plumbing; Schmidt, J.B. Co.
    D. Gigi Arts; Gordon, Jon & Associates; Schmidt, J.B. Co.; SOS Plumbing

16. The alphabetical filing order of two businesses with identical names is determined by the 16.____
    A. length of time each business has been operating
    B. addresses of the businesses
    C. last name of the company president
    D. no one of the above

17. In an alphabetical filing system, if a business name includes a number, it should be 17.____
    A. disregarded
    B. considered a number and placed at the end of an alphabetical section
    C. treated as though it were written in words and alphabetized accordingly
    D. considered a number and placed at the beginning of an alphabetical section

18. If a business name includes a contraction (such as *don't* or *it's*), how should that word be treated in an alphabetical system? 18.____
    A. Divide the word into its separate parts and treat it as two words
    B. Ignore the letters that come after the apostrophe
    C. Ignore the word that contains the contraction
    D. Ignore the apostrophe and consider all letters in the contraction

19. In what order should the parts of an address be considered when using an alphabetical filing system? 19.____
   A. City or town; state; street name; house or building number
   B. State; city or town; street name; house or building number
   C. House or building number; street name; city or town; state
   D. Street name; city or town; state

20. A business record should be cross-referenced when a(n) 20.____
   A. organization is known by an abbreviated name
   B. business has a name change because of a sale, incorporation, or other reason
   C. business is known by a *coined* or common name which differs from a dictionary spelling
   D. all of the above

21. A geographical filing system is MOST effective when 21.____
   A. location is more important than name
   B. many names or titles sound alike
   C. dealing with companies who have offices all over the world
   D. filing personal and business files

Questions 22-25.

DIRECTIONS: Questions 22 through 25 are to be answered on the basis of the list of items below, which are to be filed geographically. Organize the items geographically and then answer the questions.

I. University Press at Berkeley, U.S.
II. Maria Sanchez, Mexico City, Mexico
III. Great Expectations Ltd. in London, England
IV. Justice League, Cape Town, South Africa, Africa
V. Crown Pearls Ltd. in London, England
VI. Joseph Prasad in London, England

22. Which of the following arrangements of the items is composed according to the policy of: *Continent, Country, City, Firm or Individual Name*? 22.____
   A. V, III, IV, VI, II, I
   B. IV, V, III, VI, II, I
   C. I, IV, V, III, VI, II
   D. IV, V, III, VI, I, II

23. Which of the following files is arranged according to the policy of: *Continent, Country, City, Firm or Individual Name*? 23.____
   A. South Africa; Africa; Cape Town; Justice League
   B. Mexico; Mexico City; Maria Sanchez
   C. North America; United States; Berkeley; University Press
   D. England; Europe; London; Prasad, Joseph

24. Which of the following arrangements of the items is composed according to the policy of: *Country, City, Firm or Individual Name*? 24.____
    A. V, VI, III, II, IV, I
    B. I, V, VI, III, II, IV
    C. VI, V, III, II, IV, I
    D. V, III, VI, II, IV, I

25. Which of the following files is arranged according to a policy of: *Country, City, Firm or Individual Name*? 25.____
    A. England; London; Crown Pearls Ltd.
    B. North America; United States; Berkeley; University Press
    C. Africa; Cape Town; Justice League
    D. Mexico City; Mexico; Maria Sanchez

26. Under which of the following circumstances would a phonetic filing system be MOST effective? 26.____
    A. When the person in charge of filing can't spell very well
    B. With large files with names that sound alike
    C. With large files with names that are spelled alike
    D. All of the above

Questions 27-29.

DIRECTIONS: Questions 27 through 29 are to be answered on the basis of the following list of numerical files.

I. 391-023-100
II. 361-132-170
III. 385-732-200
IV. 381-432-150
V. 391-632-387
VI. 361-423-303
VII. 391-123-271

27. Which of the following arrangements of the files follows a consecutive-digit system? 27.____
    A. II, III, IV, I
    B. I, V, VII, III
    C. II, IV, III, I
    D. III, I, V, VII

28. Which of the following arrangements follows a terminal-digit system? 28.____
    A. I, VII, II, IV, III
    B. II, I, IV, V, VII
    C. VII, VI, V, IV, III
    D. I, IV, II, III, VII

29. Which of the following lists follows a middle-digit system? 29.____
    A. I, VII, II, VI, IV, V, III
    B. I, II, VII, IV, VI, V, III
    C. VII, II, I, III, V, VI, IV
    D. VII, I, II, IV, VI, V, III

Questions 30-31.

DIRECTIONS: Questions 30 and 31 are to be answered on the basis of the following information.

I. Reconfirm Laura Bates appointment with James Caldecort on December 12 at 9:30 A.M.
II. Laurence Kinder contact Julia Lucas on August 3 and set up a meeting for week of September 23 at 4 P.M.
III. John Lutz contact Larry Waverly on August 3 and set up appointment for September 23 at 9:30 A.M.
IV. Call for tickets for Gerry Stanton August 21 for New Jersey on September 23, flight 143 at 4:43 P.M.

30. A chronological file for the above information would be 30.____
A. IV, III, II, I B. III, II, IV, I C. IV, II, III, I D. III, I, II, IV

31. Using the above information, a chronological file for the date September 23 would be 31.____
A. II, III, IV B. III, I, IV C. III, II, IV D. IV, III, II

Questions 32-34.

DIRECTIONS: Questions 32 through 34 are to be answered on the basis of the following information.

I. Call Roger Epstein, Ashoke Naipaul, Jon Anderson, and Sara Washingon on April 19 at 1:00 P.M. to set up meeting with Alika D'Ornay for June 6 in New York.
II. Call Martin Ames before noon on April 19 to confirm afternoon meeting with Bob Greenwood on April 20th.
III. Set up meeting room at noon for 2:30 P.M. meeting on April 19th.
IV. Ashley Stanton contact Bob Greenwood at 9:00 A.M. on April 20 and set up meeting for June 6 at 8:30 A.M.
V. Carol Guiland contact Shelby Van Ness during afternoon of April 20 and set up meeting for June 6 at 10:00 A.M.
VI. Call airline and reserve tickets on June 6 for Roger Epstein trip to Denver on July 8.
VII. Meeting at 2:30 P.M. on April 19th.

32. A chronological file for all of the above information would be 32.____
A. II, I, III, VII, V, IV, VI
B. III, VII, II, I, IV, V, VI
C. III, VII, I, II, V, IV, VI
D. II, III, I, VII, IV, V, VI

33. A chronological file for the date of April 19th would be 33.____
A. II, III, VII, I B. II, III, I, VII C. VII, I, III, II D. III, VII, I, II

34. Add the following information to the file, and then create a chronological file for April 20th: VIII. April 20: 3:00 P.M. meeting between Bob Greenwood and Martin Ames. 34.____
   A. IV, V, VIII B. IV, VIII, V C. VIII, V, IV D. V, IV, VIII

35. The PRIMARY advantage of computer records over a manual system is 35.____
   A. speed of retrieval
   B. accuracy
   C. cost
   D. potential file loss

KEY (CORRECT ANSWERS)

1.	B	11.	D	21.	A	31.	C
2.	C	12.	C	22.	B	32.	D
3.	D	13.	B	23.	C	33.	B
4.	A	14.	C	24.	D	34.	A
5.	D	15.	D	25.	A	35.	A
6.	C	16.	B	26.	B		
7.	B	17.	C	27.	C		
8.	B	18.	D	28.	D		
9.	C	19.	A	29.	A		
10.	D	20.	D	30.	B		

EXAMINATION SECTION
TEST 1

DIRECTIONS: Each question or incomplete statement is followed by several suggested, answers or completions. Select the one that BEST answers the question or completes the statement. *PRINT THE LETTER OF THE CORRECT ANSWER IN THE SPACE AT THE RIGHT.*

1. Of the following, the type of water that is usually MOST suitable for mixing with normal portland cement is 1.____

   A. highly acidic water
   B. highly alkaline water
   C. water with a high sulphate content
   D. ordinary drinking water

2. Assume that the instruction manual for a machine indicates that a certain bolt must be tightened with a specified amount of force. Of the following tools, the one which should be used to tighten the bolt with the specified amount of force is a(n) ______ wrench. 2.____

   A. torque
   B. adjustable
   C. stillson
   D. combination

3. When a foreman delegates some of his work to a subordinate, the 3.____

   A. foreman retains final responsibility for the work
   B. foreman should not check on the work until it has been completed
   C. subordinate assumes full responsibility for the successful completion of the work
   D. subordinate is likely to lose interest and get less satisfaction from the work

4. The PRIMARY responsibility of a supervisor is to 4.____

   A. gain the confidence and make friends of all his subordinates
   B. get the work done properly
   C. satisfy his superior and gain his respect
   D. train the men in new methods for doing the work

Questions 5-10.

DIRECTIONS: Questions 5 through 10 are to be answered on the basis of the following information and Work Schedule Chart.

Assume that you are preparing a schedule of the work to be done by your crew of three laborers for one day. You have already planned some jobs as shown on the Work Schedule Chart. The work which remains to be scheduled is also listed below. The lunch hour for the three laborers is from 12:00 Noon to 1:00 P.M., and you may not plan any work during that period. Assume that the objective is to keep each of the three laborers occupied for a full day, except for their lunch hour. All laborers are qualified to perform the scheduled work. No changes are possible in the work already listed on the chart.

WORK SCHEDULE CHART
May 5

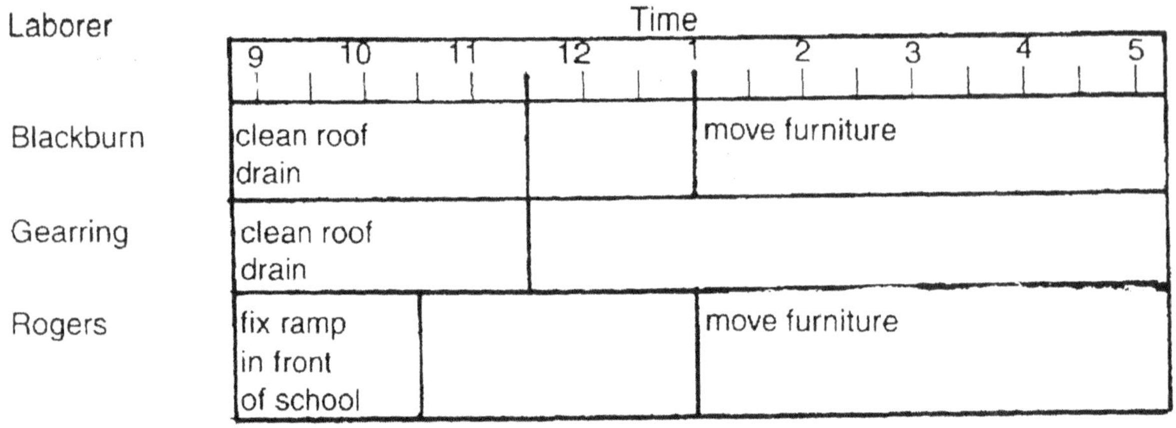
Laborer
Time
9
10
11
12
1
2
3
4
5
Blackburn
clean roof drain
move furniture
Gearring
clean roof drain
Rogers
fix ramp in front of school
move furniture

WORK REMAINING TO BE SCHEDULED FOR MAY 5:
Installing Shelves - requires 1 man for 2 hours
Repairing Window Blinds - requires 1 man for 1 hour
Changing Door Hardware - requires 1 man for 30 minutes
Cleaning Air Conditioner - requires 1 man for 1 hour
Pickup of Hardware at Supply Depot - requires 1 man for 1 1/2 hours

5. For which laborer and for what block of time would it be MOST appropriate to schedule the installing of shelves? 5.___

A. Blackburn - 11:30 A.M. - 12:00 Noon
B. Gearring - 12:30 P.M. - 1:00 P.M.
C. Rogers - 9:00 A.M. - 10:30 A.M.
D. Gearring - 1:00 P.M. - 3:00 P.M.

6. For which laborer and for what block of time would it be BEST to schedule the changing of door hardware? 6.___

A. Rogers - 9:30 A.M. - 10:00 A.M.
B. Blackburn - 11:30 A.M. - 12:00 Noon
C. Gearring - 10:00 A.M. - 10:30 A.M.
D. Rogers - 12:30 P.M. - 1:00 P.M.

7. For which laborer and for what block of time would it be MOST appropriate to schedule the repairing of window blinds? 7.___

A. Rogers - 10:30 A.M. - 11:00 A.M.
B. Gearring - 11:00 A.M. - 12:00 Noon
C. Blackburn - 4:00 P.M. - 5:00 P.M.
D. Gearring - 3:00 P.M. - 4:00 P.M.

8. For which laborer and for what block of time would it be MOST appropriate to schedule the air conditioner cleaning? 8.____

   A. Gearring - 12:30 P.M. - 1:30 P.M.
   B. Blackburn - 11:30 A.M. - 12:30 P.M.
   C. Rogers - 10:00 A.M. - 11:00 A.M.
   D. Gearring - 4:00 P.M. - 5:00 P.M.

9. For which laborer and for what block of time would it be BEST to schedule the pickup of hardware at the supply depot? 9.____

   A. Gearring - 10:30 A.M. - 11:30 A.M.
   B. Blackburn - 11:00 A.M. - 12:30 P.M.
   C. Rogers - 10:30 A.M. - 12:00 Noon
   D. Blackburn - 2:00 P.M. - 3:00 P.M.

10. After all of the work has been scheduled for May 5, which one of the following blocks of time remains unscheduled? 10.____

   A. Rogers - 10:30 A.M. - 11:30 A.M.
   B. Blackburn - 11:30 A.M. - 12:30 P.M.
   C. Gearring - 11:30 A.M. - 12:00 Noon
   D. Rogers - 12:30 P.M. - 1:00 P.M.

Questions 11-20.

DIRECTIONS: Questions 11 through 20 are to be answered solely on the basis of the following chart. Note that each driver works a 9 A.M. to 5 P.M. shift, and is allowed one hour for lunch each day.

SCHEDULE OF PICKUPS AND DELIVERIES
April 12

Driver	Activity	Items	Location	Activity Time Start End	Odometer Reading Start End
McCoy	Pickup	87 refrigerators	163 Bway, N.Y.C.	9:00 12:30	27,328 27,361
	Pickup	17 desks	80 Park Ave. So., N.Y.C.	1:30 2:45	
	Pickup	178 chairs	235 E. 43 St. N.Y.C.	2:45 4:15	
Hafner	Delivery	Oak paneling 50 sheets 11' x 15'	4309 Van Cortlandt Pkwy, Bronx	9:00 11:00	15,019 15,067
	Pickup	50 desks	4309 Van Cortlandt Pkwy, Bronx	11:00 12:15	
	Delivery	20 glass partitions 5' x 7 1/2'	1059 Murdock Ave., Bronx	1:15 3:45	
O'Neil	Delivery	30 shelves 2' x 4'	605 Lafayette St., Bklyn	9:00 10:45	32,546 32,575
	Delivery	17 file cabinets	54 Boerum St. Bklyn	10:45 1:15	
	Pickup	42 desks	430 Fulton St., Bklyn	2:15 4:25	
Tobin	Delivery	37 chairs	809 Kingston Ave., Bklyn	9:00 10:50	33,489 33,510
	Delivery	20 sheets 1/2" plywood 4' x 8'	1072 Bedford Ave., Bklyn	10:50 12:20	
	Delivery	15 glass partitions 5' x 7 1/2'	195 Wilson Ave., Bklyn	1:20 3:20	
Guzman	Pickup	20 glass partitions 6' x 7'	135 Barclay St., N.Y.C.	9:00 11:45	12,967 13,004
	Pickup	oak paneling 30 sheets 11' x 15'	192 Varick St., N.Y.C.	11:45 1:15	
	Pickup	10 file cabinets	72 Pine St. , N.Y.C.	2:15 4:00	

11. The average amount of time spent by O'Neil on each of his activities was APPROXIMATELY ______ hour(s) ______ minutes. 11.___

A. 1; 45 B. 2; 10 C. 2; 45 D. 3; 10

12. At which one of the following locations was the latest pickup started? 12.___

A. 430 Fulton St., Brooklyn
B. 72 Pine Street, N.Y.C.
C. 195 Wilson Avenue, Brooklyn
D. 235 East 43rd Street, N.Y.C.

13. Which one of the following activities was Tobin performing at 11:00 A.M.? 13.___

A. Picking up chairs
B. Delivering glass partitions
C. Picking up desks
D. Delivering plywood sheets

14. The name of the driver who picked up material and delivered material at the same location is 14.____

A. McCoy B. Hafner C. O'Neil D. Tobin

15. The name of the driver who picked up 20 glass partitions is 15.____

A. McCoy B. Hafner C. Tobin D. Guzman

16. According to the chart, the driver who traveled the GREATEST number of miles is 16.____

A. McCoy B. Hafner C. O'Neil D. Guzman

17. According to the chart, which activities were among those performed by Hafner? He 17.____

A. picked up 50 sheets of oak paneling and delivered 50 desks
B. picked up 20 glass partitions and delivered 50 desks
C. delivered 50 desks and 20 glass partitions
D. delivered 50 sheets of oak paneling and 20 glass partitions

18. According to the chart, which drivers began their lunch hours after 1:00 P.M.? 18.____

A. McCoy and Hafner
B. Hafner and O'Neil
C. O'Neil and Guzman
D. Tobin and Guzman

19. The average number of miles traveled by all trucks on April 12 is MOST NEARLY 19.____

A. 33 B. 34 C. 37 D. 39

20. According to the chart, which driver spent the GREATEST period of time on a single activity? 20.____

A. Tobin B. Guzman C. Hafner D. McCoy

KEY(CORRECT ANSWERS)

1.	D	11.	B
2.	A	12.	D
3.	A	13.	D
4.	B	14.	B
5.	D	15.	D
6.	B	16.	B
7.	D	17.	D
8.	D	18.	C
9.	C	19.	B
10.	C	20.	D

TEST 2

DIRECTIONS: Each question or incomplete statement is followed by several suggested answers or completions. Select the one that BEST answers the question or completes the statement. *PRINT THE LETTER OF THE CORRECT ANSWER IN THE SPACE AT THE RIGHT.*

Questions 1-10.

DIRECTIONS: Questions 1 through 10 are based upon equipment and articles. These are items which a foreman may be called upon to move between two distant locations. There are many considerations that govern the correct handling and moving of these articles and, depending upon the characteristics of the individual item, usually there will be one factor that will have the greatest influence on the decision as to how the item is to be handled, the equipment that might be needed, the time of delivery, or the number of employees needed to complete the task satisfactorily.
For each question, select the one choice which represents the factor that should require PRIMARY consideration.

1. The PRIMARY factor to be considered when moving 100 automotive maintenance work tables is: 1.____

   A. Can these articles be disassembled?
   B. What is the monetary cost of each table?
   C. How durable is each table?
   D. Are the tables in used or new condition?

2. The PRIMARY factor to be considered when moving tables with folding legs is the 2.____

   A. number of tables to be moved
   B. time each laborer takes to fold the set of pairs of legs under each table
   C. use to be made of the tables
   D. value of each table

3. The PRIMARY factor to be considered when moving 200 chairs is the 3.____

   A. capability to stack one chair upon another
   B. practicability of disassembling each chair into component parts
   C. special wrapping required for each chair
   D. physical strength required of the movers

4. The PRIMARY factor to be considered when moving 25 swivel chairs is the 4.____

   A. knowledge that the frame is of steel construction
   B. identification or labeling of each chair
   C. physical condition of the material on each chair
   D. condition of the casters on each chair

5. The PRIMARY factor to be considered when moving fans is the 5.____

   A. requirement that the fans be in operating condition before delivery takes place
   B. fact that replacements are difficult to obtain in cases of loss in shipment

C. fact that the size and bulk of the fan can be accommodated by available transport vehicles
D. absence of wire guards around the fan blades which constitutes a safety hazard

6. The PRIMARY factor to be considered when moving 35 gate valves is the 6.____

A. past experience that the men assigned have had in moving other kinds of metal equipment
B. size and weight of each valve
C. number of forms the foreman must complete
D. probable use by the mechanic at the site

7. The PRIMARY factor to be considered when moving 100 lockers from storage to a school gym is: 7.____

A. Can the lockers be disassembled?
B. Are the lockers to be installed in multiples of 3 units or in multiples of 6 units?
C. Are the lockers new or used?
D. What is the scrap value of lockers?

8. The PRIMARY factor to be considered when moving typewriters is the 8.____

A. provision whether the typewriters are going to be sold or put into storage
B. determination by the foreman as to what parts are likely to be bent or thrown out of order in the process of moving
C. cost of replacement parts in the event of damage to the typewriters
D. type of typewriter; is it manual or electric?

9. The PRIMARY factor to be considered when moving a compressor is the 9.____

A. absence of a guard enclosing the moving parts of the compressor
B. degree of close attention the foreman must devote to directing the process of moving
C. operating instructions furnished by the manufacturer of the compressor
D. physical dimensions and weight of the compressor

10. The PRIMARY factor to be considered when moving file cabinets from one room to another on the same floor is: 10.____

A. Can the cabinets be locked?
B. Are the cabinets letter or legal size?
C. How many drawers are in each file cabinet?
D. What is the total number of file cabinets to be moved?

Questions 11-13.

DIRECTIONS: A foreman is asked to write a report on the incident described in the following passage. Answer Questions 11 through 13 based on the following information.

On March 10, Henry Moore, a laborer, was in the process of transferring some equipment from the machine shop to the third floor. He was using a dolly to perform this task and, as he was wheeling the material through the machine shop, laborer Bob Greene called to him. As Henry turned to respond to Bob, he jammed the dolly into Larry Mantell's leg, knocking Larry down in the process and causing the heavy drill that Larry was holding to fall on Larry's foot. Larry started rubbing his foot and then, infuriated, jumped up and punched Henry in the jaw. The force of the blow drove Henry's head back against the wall. Henry did not fight back; he appeared to be dazed. An ambulance was called to take Henry to the hospital, and the ambulance attendant told the foreman that it appeared likely that Henry had suffered a concussion. Larry's injuries consisted of some bruises, but he refused medical attention.

11. An adequate report of the above incident should give as minimum information the names of the persons involved, the names of the witnesses, the date and the time that each event took place, and the 11.____

    A. names of the ambulance attendants
    B. names of all the employees working in the machine shop
    C. location where the accident occurred
    D. nature of the previous safety training each employee had been given

12. The only one of the following which is NOT a fact is: 12.____

    A. Bob called to Henry
    B. Larry suffered a concussion
    C. Larry rubbed his foot
    D. The incident took place in the machine shop

13. Which of the following would be the MOST accurate summary of the incident for the foreman to put in his report of the accident? 13.____

    A. Larry Mantell punched Henry Moore because a drill fell on his foot and he was angry. Then Henry fell and suffered a concussion.
    B. Henry Moore accidentally jammed a dolly into Larry Mantell's foot, knocking Larry down. Larry punched Henry, pushing him into the wall and causing him to bang his head against the wall.
    C. Bob Greene called Henry Moore. A dolly then jammed into Larry Mantell and knocked him down. Larry punched Henry who tripped and suffered some bruises. An ambulance was called.
    D. A drill fell on Larry Mantell's foot. Larry jumped up suddenly and punched Henry Moore and pushed him into the wall. Henry may have suffered a concussion as a result of falling.

14. It is said that the morale of a staff is usually a good indication of the quality of leadership exercised by the supervisor of the staff. Of the following, the BEST indication of high morale among a staff is: 14.____

    A. Disciplinary actions against members of the staff are rare
    B. It is seldom necessary for the staff to work overtime
    C. The staff is seldom late in reporting for work
    D. The staff subordinates personal desires in favor of group objectives

15. In starting a work simplification study, the one of the following steps that should be taken FIRST is to 15.____

    A. break the work down into its elements
    B. draw up a chart of operations

C. enlist the interest and cooperation of the personnel
D. suggest alternative procedures

16. Of the following, the MOST important value of a manual of procedures is that it USUALLY 16.____

A. eliminates the need for on-the-job training
B. decreases the span of control which can be exercised by individual supervisory personnel
C. outlines methods of operation for ready reference
D. provides concrete examples of work previously performed by employees

17. In conducting an analysis of the flow of work in a store-roori or storehouse, it is USUALLY advisable to begin the analysis with the 17.____

A. supervisory work
B. technical work
C. work of a major routine nature
D. work of a minor routine nature

18. When planning a staff development program for his subordinates, the one of the following which it is usually MOST important for the foreman to consider is the 18.____

A. chief storekeeping problems of the department
B. common needs of his subordinates in terms of the daily work situation
C. evaluation of similar training programs offered by other departments
D. time available for classes and meetings

19. Reprimanding a subordinate when he has done something wrong should be done PRIMARILY in order to 19.____

A. deter others from similar acts
B. improve the subordinate's future performance
C. maintain discipline
D. uphold departmental rules

20. You find that delivery of a certain item cannot possibly be nade to a using agency by the date the using agency requested. Of the following, the MOST advisable course of action for you to take FIRST is to 20.____

A. cancel the order and inform the using agency
B. discuss the problem with the using agency
C. notify the using agency to obtain the item through direct purchase
D. schedule the delivery for the earliest possible date

KEY (CORRECT ANSWERS)

1. A
2. A
3. A
4. D
5. C

6. B
7. A
8. B
9. D
10. D

11. C
12. B
13. B
14. D
15. C

16. C
17. C
18. B
19. B
20. B

EXAMINATION SECTION

TEST 1

DIRECTIONS: Each question or incomplete statement is followed by several suggested answers or completions. Select the one that BEST answers the question or completes the statement. *PRINT THE LETTER OF THE CORRECT ANSWER IN THE SPACE AT THE RIGHT.*

1. The one of the following which is the CHIEF reason for the difference between the administration of justice agencies and that of other units in public administration is that 1.____
   A. correctional institutions are concerned with security
   B. some defendants are proven to be innocent after trial
   C. the administration of justice is more complicated than other aspects of public administration
   D. correctional institutions produce services their clients or customers fail to understand or ask for

2. Of the following, the MOST important reason why employees resist change is that 2.____
   A. they have not received adequate training in preparation for the change
   B. experience has shown that when new ideas don't work, employees get blamed and not the individuals responsible for the new ideas
   C. new ideas and methods almost always represent a threat to the security of the individuals involved
   D. new ideas often are not practical and disrupt operations unnecessarily

3. Stress situations are ideal for building up a backlog of knowledge about an employee's behavior. Not only does it inform the supervisor of many aspects of a person's behavior patterns, but it is also vitally important to have foreknowledge of how people behave under stress. 3.____
   The one of the following which is NOT implied by this passage is that
   A. a person under stress may give some indication of his unsuitability for work in an institution
   B. putting people under stress is the best means of determining their usual patterns of behavior
   C. stress situations may give important clues about performance in the service
   D. there is a need to know about a person's reaction to situations *when the chips are down*

4. There are situations requiring a supervisor to give direct orders to subordinates assigned to work under the direct control of other supervisors. 4.____
   Under which of the following conditions would this shift of command responsibility be MOST appropriate?
   A. Emergency operations require the cooperative action of two or more organizational units.

B. One of the other supervisors is not doing his job, thus defeating the goals of the organization.
C. The subordinates are performing their assigned tasks in the absence of their own supervisor.
D. The subordinates ask a superior officer who is not their own supervisor how to perform an assignment given them by their supervisor.

5. The one of the following which BEST differentiates staff supervision from line supervision is that 5.____
   A. staff supervision has the authority to immediately correct a line subordinate's action
   B. staff supervision is an advisory relationship
   C. line supervision goes beyond the normal boundaries of direct supervision within a command
   D. line supervision does not report findings and make recommendations

6. Decision-making is a rational process calling for a *suspended judgment* by the supervisor until all the facts have been ascertained and analyzed, and the consequences of alternative courses of action studied; then the decision maker 6.____
   A. acts as both judge and jury and selects what he believes to be the best of the alternative plans
   B. consults with those who will be most directly involved to obtain a recommendation as to the most appropriate course of action
   C. reviews the facts which he has already analyzed, reduces his thoughts to writing, and selects that course of action which can have the fewest negative consequences if his thinking contains an error
   D. stops, considers the matter for at least a 24-hour period, before referring it to a superior for evaluation

7. Decision-making can be defined as the 7.____
   A. delegation of authority and responsibility to persons capable of performing their assigned duties with moderate or little supervision
   B. imposition of a supervisor's decision upon a work group
   C. technique of selecting the course of action with the most desired consequences, and the least undesired or unexpected consequence
   D. process principally concerned with improvement of procedures

8. A supervisor who is not well-motivated and has no desire to accept basic responsibilities will 8.____
   A. compromise to the extent of permitting poor performance for lengthy periods without correction
   B. get good performance from his work group if the employees are satisfied with their pay and other working conditions
   C. not have marginal workers in his work group if the work is interesting
   D. perform adequately as long as the work of his group consists of routine operations

9. A supervisor is more than a bond or connecting link between two levels of employees. He has joint responsibility which must be shared with both management and with the work group. 9.____
Of the following, the item which BEST expresses the meaning of this statement is:
   A. A supervisor works with both management and the work group and must reconcile the differences between them.
   B. In management, the supervisor is solely concerned with efforts directing the work of his subordinates.
   C. The supervisory role is basically that of a liaison man between management and the work force.
   D. What a supervisor says and does when confronted with day-to-day problems depends upon is level in the organization.

10. Operations research is the observation of operations in business or government, and it utilizes both hypotheses and controlled experiments to determine the outcome of decisions. In effect, it reproduces the future impact on the decision in a clinical environment suited to intensive study. 10.____
Operations research has
   A. been more promising than applied research in the ascertaining of knowledge for the purpose of decision-making
   B. never been amenable to fact analysis on the grand scale
   C. not been used extensively in government
   D. proven to be the only rational and logical approach to decision-making on long-range problems

11. Assume that a civilian makes a complaint regarding the behavior of a certain worker to the supervisor of the worker. The supervisor regards the complaint as unjustified and unreasonable. 11.____
In this circumstances, the supervisor
   A. must make a written note of the complaint and forward it through channels to the unit or individual responsible for complaint investigations
   B. should assure the complainant that disciplinary action will be appropriate to the seriousness of the alleged offense
   C. should immediately summon the worker if he is available so that the latter may attempt to straighten out the difficulty
   D. should inform the complainant that his complaint appears to be unjustified and unreasonable

12. Modern management usually establishes a personal history folder for an employee at the time of hiring. Disciplinary matters appear in such personal history folders. Employees do not like the idea of disciplinary actions appearing in their permanent personal folders. 12.____
Authorities believe that
   A. after a few years have passed since the commission of the infraction, disciplinary actions should be removed from folders
   B. disciplinary actions should remain in folders; it is not the records but the use of records that requires detailed study

C. most personnel have not had disciplinary action taken against them and would resent the removal of disciplinary actions for such folders
D. there is no point in removing disciplinary actions from personal history folders since employees who have been guilty of infractions should not be allowed to forget their infractions

13. While supervisors should not fear the acceptance of responsibility, they 13.____
A. generally seek out responsibility that subordinates should exercise, particularly when the supervisors do not have sufficient work to do
B. must be on guard against the abuse of authority that often accompanies the acceptance of total responsibility
C. should avoid responsibility that is customarily exercised by their superiors
D. who are anxious for promotions accept responsibility but do not exercise the authority warranted by the responsibility

14. Planning is part of the decision-making process. By planning is meant the development of details of alternative plans of action. 14.____
The key to *effective* planning is
A. careful research to determine whether a tentative plan has been tried at some time in the past
B. participation by employees in planning, preferably those employees who will be involved in putting the selected plan into action
C. speed; poor plans can be discarded after they are put into effect while good plans usually are not put into effect because of delays
D. writing the plan up in considerable detail and then forwarding the plan, through channels, to the executive officer having final approval of the plan

15. Equating strict discipline with punitive measures and lax discipline with rehabilitation creates a false dichotomy. 15.____
The one of the statements given below that would BEST follow from the belief expressed in this statement is that discipline
A. is important for treatment
B. militates against treatment programs
C. is not an important consideration in institutions where effective rehabilitation programs prevail
D. minimizes the need for punitive measures if it is strict

16. If training starts at the lower level of command, it is like planting a seed in tilled ground but removing the sun and rain. Seeds cannot grow unless they have help from above. 16.____
Of the following, the MOST appropriate conclusion to be drawn from this statement is that
A. the head of an institution may not delegate authority for the planning of an institutional training program for staff
B. on-the-job training is better than formalized training courses
C. regularly scheduled training courses must be planned in advance
D. staff training is the responsibility of higher levels of comman

17. The one of the following that BEST describes the meaning of *in-service staff training* is: 17.____
    A. The training of personnel who are below average in performance
    B. The training given to each employee throughout his employment
    C. The training of staff only in their own specialized fields
    D. Classroom training where the instructor and employees develop a positive and productive relationship leading to improved efficiency on the job

18. All bureau personnel should be concerned about, and involved in, public relations. 18.____
    Of the following, the MOST important reason for this statement is that
    A. an institution is an agency of the government supported by public funds and responsible to the public
    B. institutions are places of public business and, therefore, the public is interested in them
    C. some personnel need publicity in order to advance
    D. personnel sometimes need publicity in order to ensure that their grievances are acted upon by higher authority

19. The MOST important factor in establishing a disciplinary policy in an organization is 19.____
    A. consistency of application
    B. strict supervisors
    C. strong enforcement
    D. the degree of toughness or laxity

20. The FIRST step in planning a program is to 20.____
    A. clearly define the objectives
    B. estimate the costs
    C. hire a program director
    D. solicit funds

21. The PRIMARY purpose of control in an organization is to 21.____
    A. punish those who do not do their job well
    B. get people to do what is necessary to achieve an objective
    C. develop clearly stated rules and regulations
    D. regulate expenditures

22. The UNDERLYING principle of *sound* administration is to 22.____
    A. base administration on investigation of facts
    B. have plenty of resources available
    C. hire a strong administrator
    D. establish a broad policy

23. An IMPORTANT aspect to keep in mind during the decision-making process is that 23.____
    A. all possible alternatives for attaining goals should be sought out and considered
    B. considering various alternatives only leads to confusion
    C. once a decision has been made, it cannot be retracted
    D. there is only one correct method to reach any goal

24. Implementation of accountability requires 24.____
    A. a leader who will not hesitate to take punitive action
    B. an established system of communication from the bottom to the top
    C. explicit directives from leaders
    D. too much expense to justify it

25. The CHIEF danger of a decentralized control system is that 25.____
    A. excessive reports and communications will be generated
    B. problem areas may not be detected readily
    C. the expense will become prohibitive
    D. this will result in too many *chiefs*

KEY (CORRECT ANSWERS)

1.	D	11.	D
2.	C	12.	A
3.	B	13.	B
4.	A	14.	B
5.	B	15.	A
6.	A	16.	D
7.	C	17.	B
8.	A	18.	A
9.	A	19.	A
10.	C	20.	A
21.	B		
22.	A		
23.	A		
24.	B		
25.	B		

TEST 2

DIRECTIONS: Each question or incomplete statement is followed by several suggested answers or completions. Select the one that BEST answers the question or completes the statement. *PRINT THE LETTER OF THE CORRECT ANSWER IN THE SPACE AT THE RIGHT.*

1. When giving orders to his subordinates, a certain supervisor often includes information as to why the work is necessary. 1.____
This approach by the supervisor is GENERALLY
   A. *inadvisable*, since it appears that he is avoiding responsibility and wishes to blame his superiors
   B. *inadvisable*, since it creates the impression that he is trying to impress the subordinates with his importance
   C. *advisable*, since it serves to motivate the subordinates by giving them a reason for wanting to do the work
   D. *advisable*, since it shows that he is knowledgeable and is in control of his assignments

2. Some supervisors often ask capable, professional subordinates to get some work done with questions such as: *Mary, would you try to complete that work today?* 2.____
The use of such request orders USUALLY
   A. gets results which are as good as or better than results from direct orders
   B. shows the supervisor to be weak and lowers the respect of his subordinates
   C. provokes resentment as compared to the use of direct orders
   D. leads to confusion as to the proper procedure to follow when carrying out orders

3. Assume that a supervisor, because of an emergency when time was essential, and in the absence of his immediate superior, went out of the chain of command to get a decision from a higher level. 3.____
It would consequently be MOST appropriate for the immediate superior to
   A. reprimand him for his action, since the long-range consequences are far more detrimental than the immediate gain
   B. encourage him to use this method, since the chain of command is an outmoded and discredited system which inhibits productive work
   C. order him to refrain from any repetition of this action in the future
   D. support him as long as he informed the superior of the action at the earliest opportunity

4. A supervisor gave instructions which he knew were somewhat complex to a subordinate. He then asked the subordinate to repeat the instructions to him. 4.____
The supervisor's decision to have the subordinate repeat the instructions was
   A. *good practice*, mainly because the subordinate would realize the importance of carefully following instructions

B. *poor practice*, mainly because the supervisor should have given the employee time to ponder the instructions, and then, if necessary, to ask questions
C. *good practice*, mainly because the supervisor could see whether the subordinate had any apparent problem in understanding the instructions
D. *poor practice*, mainly because the subordinate should not be expected to have the same degree of knowledge as the supervisor

5. Supervisors and subordinates must successfully communicate with each other in order to work well together. 5.____
Which of the following statements concerning communication of this type is CORRECT?
A. When speaking to his subordinates, a supervisor should make every effort to appear knowledgeable about all aspects of their work.
B. Written communications should be prepared by the supervisor at his own level of comprehension.
C. The average employee tends to give meaning to communication according to his personal interpretation.
D. The effective supervisor communicates as much information as he has available to anyone who is interested.

6. A supervisor should be aware of situations in which it is helpful to put his orders to his subordinates in writing. 6.____
Which of the following situations would MOST likely call for a written order rather than an oral order?
The order
A. gives complicated instructions which vary from ordinary practice
B. involves the performance of duties for which the subordinate is responsible
C. directs subordinates to perform duties similar to those which they performed in the recent past
D. concerns a matter that must be promptly completed or dealt with

7. Assume that a supervisor discovers that a false rumor about possible layoffs has spread among his subordinates through the grapevine. 7.____
Of the following, the BEST way for the supervisor to deal with this situation is to
A. use the grapevine to leak accurate information
B. call a meeting to provide information and to answer questions
C. post a notice on the bulletin board denying the rumor
D. institute procedures designed to eliminate the grapevine

8. Communications in an organization with many levels becomes subject to different interpretations at each level and have a tendency to become distorted. The more levels there are in an organization, the greater the likelihood that the final recipient of a communication will get the wrong message. 8.____
The one of the following statements which BEST supports the foregoing viewpoint is:
A. Substantial communications problems exist at high management levels in organizations.

B. There is a relationship in an organization between the number of hierarchical levels and interference with communications.
C. An opportunity should be given to subordinates at all levels to communicate their views with impunity.
D. In larger organizations, there tends to be more interference with downward communications than with upward communications.

9. A subordinate comes to you, his supervisor, to ask a detailed question about a new agency directive; however, you do not know the answer. 9.____
Of the following, the MOST helpful response to give the subordinate is to
A. point out that since your own supervisor has failed to keep you informed of this matter, it is probably unimportant
B. give the most logical interpretation you can, based on your best judgment
C. ask him to raise the question with other supervisors until he finds one who knows the answer, then let you know also
D. explain that you do not know and assure him that you will get the information for him

10. The traditional view of management theory is that communication in an organization should follow the table of organization. A newer theory holds that timely communication often requires bypassing certain steps in the hierarchical chain. 10.____
However, the MAIN advantage of using formal channels of communication within an organization is that
A. an employee is thereby restricted in his relationships to his immediate superior and his immediate subordinates
B. information is thereby transmitted to everyone who should be informed
C. the organization will have an appeal channel, or a mechanism by which subordinates can go over their superior's head
D. employees are thereby encouraged to exercise individual initiative

11. It is unfair to hold subordinates responsible for the performance of duties for which they do not have the requisite authority. 11.____
When this is done, it violates the principle that
A. responsibility cannot be greater than that implied by delegated authority
B. responsibility should be greater than that implied by delegated authority
C. authority cannot be greater than that implied by delegated responsibility
D. authority should be greater than that implied by delegated responsibility

12. Assume that a supervisor wishes to delegate some tasks to a capable subordinate. 12.____
It would be MOST in keeping with the principles of delegation for the supervisor to
A. ask another supervisor who is experienced in the delegated tasks to evaluate the subordinate's work from time to time
B. monitor continually the subordinate's performance by carefully reviewing his work

C. request experienced employees to submit peer ratings of the work of the subordinate
D. tell the subordinates what problems are likely to be encountered and specify which problems to report on

13. There are three types of leadership: *autocratic*, in which the leader makes the decisions and seeks compliance from his subordinates; *democratic*, in which the leader consults with his subordinate and lets them help set policy; and *free rein*, in which the leader acts as an information center and exercises minimum control over his subordinates. 13.____
A supervisor can be MOST effective if he decides to
A. use democratic leadership techniques exclusively
B. avoid the use of autocratic leadership techniques entirely
C. employ the three types of leadership according to the situation
D. rely mainly on autocratic leadership techniques

14. During a busy period of work, Employee A asked his supervisor for leave in order to take an ordinary vacation. The supervisor denied the request. The following day, Employee B asked for leave during the same period because his wife had just gone to the hospital for an indeterminate stay and he had family matters to tend to. 14.____
Of the following, the BEST way for the supervisor to deal with Employee B's request is to
A. grant the request and give the reason to the other employee
B. suggest that the employee make his request to higher management
C. delay the request immediately since granting it would show favoritism
D. defer any decision until the duration of the hospital stay is determined

15. Assume that you are a supervisor and that a subordinate tells you he has a grievance. 15.____
In general, you should FIRST
A. move the grievance forward in order to get a prompt decision
B. discourage this type of behavior on the part of subordinates
C. attempt to settle the grievance
D. refer the subordinate to the personnel office

16. A supervisor may have available a large variety of rewards he can use to motivate his subordinates. However, some supervisors choose the wrong rewards. 16.____
A supervisor is MOST likely to make such a mistake if he
A. appeals to a subordinate's desire to be well regarded by his co-workers
B. assumes that the subordinate's goals and preferences are the same as his own
C. conducts in-depth discussions with a subordinate in order to discover his preference
D. limits incentives to those rewards which he is authorized to provide or to recommend

17. Employee performance appraisal is open to many kinds of errors. When a supervisor is preparing such an appraisal, he is MOST likely to commit an error if 17.____
    A. employees are indifferent to the consequences of their performance appraisals
    B. the entire period for which the evaluation is being made is taken into consideration
    C. standard measurement criteria are used as performance benchmarks
    D. personal characteristics of employees which are not job-related are given weight

18. Assume that a supervisor finds that a report prepared by an employee is unsatisfactory and should be done over. Which of the following should the supervisor do? 18.____
    A. Give the report to another employee who can complete it properly
    B. Have the report done over by the same employee after successfully training him
    C. Hold a meeting to train all the employees so as not to single out the employee who performed unsatisfactory
    D. Accept the report so as not to discourage the employee and then make the corrections himself

19. Employees sometimes wish to have personal advice and counseling, in confidence, about their job-related problems. These problems may include such concerns as health matters, family difficulties, alcoholism, debts, emotional disturbances, etc. Such assistance is BEST provided through 19.____
    A. maintenance of an exit interview program to find reasons for, and solutions to, turn-over problems
    B. arrangements for employees to discuss individual problems informally outside normal administrative channels
    C. procedures which allow employees to submit anonymous inquiries to the personnel department
    D. special hearing committees consisting of top management in addition to immediate supervisors

20. An employee is always a member of some unit of the formal organization. He may also be a member of an informal work group. With respect to employee productivity and job satisfaction, the informal work group can MOST accurately be said to 20.____
    A. have no influence of any kind on its members
    B. influence its members negatively only
    C. influence its members positively only
    D. influence its members negatively or positively

21. In order to encourage employees to make suggestions, many public agencies have employee suggestion programs. What is the MAJOR benefit of such a program to the agency as a whole? 21.____

It
A. brings existing or future problems to management's attention
B. reduces the number of minor accidents
C. requires employees to share in decision-making responsibilities
D. reveals employees who have inadequate job knowledge

22. Assume that you have been asked to interview a seemingly shy applicant for a temporary position in your department. 22.____
For you to ask the kinds of questions that begin with *What, Where, Why, When, Who, and How*, is
A. *good practice*; it informs the applicant that he must conform to the requirements of the department
B. *poor practice*; it exceeds the extent and purpose of an initial interview
C. *good practice*; it encourages the applicant to talk to a greater extent
D. *poor practice*; it encourages the applicant to dominate the discussion

23. In recent years, job enlargement or job enrichment has tended to replace job simplification. 23.____
Those who advocate job enrichment or enlargement consider it *desirable* CHIEFLY because
A. it allows supervisors to control closely the activities of subordinates
B. it produces greater job satisfaction through reduction of responsibility
C. most employees prefer to avoid work which is new and challenging
D. positions with routinized duties are unlikely to provide job satisfaction

24. Job rotation is a training method in which an employee temporarily changes places with another employee of equal rank. 24.____
What is usually the MAIN purpose of job rotation? To
A. politely remove the person being rotated from an unsuitable assignment
B. increase skills and provide broader experience
C. prepare the person being rotated for a permanent change
D. test the skills of the person being rotated

25. There are several principles that a supervisor needs to know if he is to deal adequately with his training responsibilities. 25.____
Which of the following is usually NOT a principle of training?
A. People should be trained according to their individual needs.
B. People can learn by being told or shown how to do work but best of all by doing work under guidance.
C. People can be easily trained even if they have no desire to learn.
D. Training should be planned, scheduled, executed, and evaluated systematically.

KEY (CORRECT ANSWERS)

1. C
2. A
3. D
4. C
5. C

6. A
7. B
8. B
9. D
10. B

11. A
12. D
13. C
14. A
15. C

16. B
17. D
18. B
19. B
20. D

21. A
22. C
23. D
24. B
25. C

PHILOSOPHY, PRINCIPLES, PRACTICES, AND TECHNICS OF SUPERVISION, ADMINISTRATION, MANAGEMENT, AND ORGANIZATION

TABLE OF CONTENTS

PHILOSOPHY, PRINCIPLES, PRACTICES, AND TECHNICS
OF
SUPERVISION, ADMINISTRATION, MANAGEMENT, AND ORGANIZATION

MEANING OF SUPERVISION

The extension of the democratic philosophy has been accompanied by an extension in the scope of supervision. Modern leaders and supervisors no longer think of supervision in the narrow sense of being confined chiefly to visiting employees, supplying materials, or rating the staff. They regard supervision as being intimately related to all the concerned agencies of society, they speak of the supervisor's function in terms of "growth," rather than the "improvement" of employees.

This modern concept of supervision may be defined as follows: Supervision is leadership and the development of leadership within groups which are cooperatively engaged in inspection, research, training, guidance, and evaluation.

THE OLD AND THE NEW SUPERVISION

TRADITIONAL
1. Inspection
2. Focused on the employee
3. Visitation
4. Random and haphazard
5. Imposed and authoritarian
6. One person usually

MODERN
1. Study and analysis
2. Focused on aims, materials, methods, supervisors, employees, environment
3. Demonstrations, intervisitation, workshops, directed reading, bulletins, etc.
4. Definitely organized and planned (scientific)
5. Cooperative and democratic
6. Many persons involved (creative)

THE EIGHT (8) BASIC PRINCIPLES OF THE NEW SUPERVISION

I. Principle of Responsibility
Authority to act and responsibility for acting must be joined.
   A. If you give responsibility, give authority.
   B. Define employee duties clearly.
   C. Protect employees from criticism by others.
   D. Recognize the rights as well as obligations of employees.
   E. Achieve the aims of a democratic society insofar as it is possible within the area of your work.
   F. Establish a situation favorable to training and learning.
   G. Accept ultimate responsibility for everything done in your section, unit, office, division, department.
   H. Good administration and good supervision are inseparable.

II. Principle of Authority

The success of the supervisor is measured by the extent to which the power of authority is not used.

A. Exercise simplicity and informality in supervision
B. Use the simplest machinery of supervision
C. If it is good for the organization as a whole, it is probably justified.
D. Seldom be arbitrary or authoritative.
E. Do not base your work on the power of position or of personality.
F. Permit and encourage the free expression of opinions.

III. Principle of Self-Growth

The success of the supervisor is measured by the extent to which, and the speed with which, he is no longer needed.

A. Base criticism on principles, not on specifics.
B. Point out higher activities to employees.
C. Train for self-thinking by employees to meet new situations.
D. Stimulate initiative, self-reliance, and individual responsibility
E. Concentrate on stimulating the growth of employees rather than on removing defects.

IV. Principle of Individual Worth

Respect for the individual is a paramount consideration in supervision.

A. Be human and sympathetic in dealing with employees.
B. Don't nag about things to be done.
C. Recognize the individual differences among employees and seek opportunities to permit best expression of each personality.

V. Principle of Creative Leadership

The best supervision is that which is not apparent to the employee.

A. Stimulate, don't drive employees to creative action.
B. Emphasize doing good things.
C. Encourage employees to do what they do best.
D. Do not be too greatly concerned with details of subject or method.
E. Do not be concerned exclusively with immediate problems and activities.
F. Reveal higher activities and make them both desired and maximally possible.
G. Determine procedures in the light of each situation but see that these are derived from a sound basic philosophy.
H. Aid, inspire, and lead so as to liberate the creative spirit latent in all good employees.

VI. Principle of Success and Failure

There are no unsuccessful employees, only unsuccessful supervisors who have failed to give proper leadership.

A. Adapt suggestions to the capacities, attitudes, and prejudices of employees.
B. Be gradual, be progressive, be persistent.
C. Help the employee find the general principle; have the employee apply his own problem to the general principle.
D. Give adequate appreciation for good work and honest effort.
E. Anticipate employee difficulties and help to prevent them.
F. Encourage employees to do the desirable things they will do anyway.
G. Judge your supervision by the results it secures.

VII. Principle of Science
Successful supervision is scientific, objective, and experimental. It is based on facts, not on prejudices.
A. Be cumulative in results.
B. Never divorce your suggestions from the goals of training.
C. Don't be impatient of results.
D. Keep all matters on a professional, not a personal, level.
E. Do not be concerned exclusively with immediate problems and activities.
F. Use objective means of determining achievement and rating where possible.

VIII. Principle of Cooperation
Supervision is a cooperative enterprise between supervisor and employee.
A. Begin with conditions as they are.
B. Ask opinions of all involved when formulating policies.
C. Organization is as good as its weakest link.
D. Let employees help to determine policies and department programs.
E. Be approachable and accessible—physically and mentally.
F. Develop pleasant social relationships.

WHAT IS ADMINISTRATION

Administration is concerned with providing the environment, the material facilities, and the operational procedures that will promote the maximum growth and development of supervisors and employees. (Organization is an aspect and a concomitant of administration.)

There is no sharp line of demarcation between supervision and administration; these functions are intimately interrelated and, often, overlapping. They are complementary activities.

I. Practices Commonly Classed as "Supervisory"
A. Conducting employees' conferences
B. Visiting sections, units, offices, divisions, departments
C. Arranging for demonstrations
D. Examining plans
E. Suggesting professional reading
F. Interpreting bulletins
G. Recommending in-service training courses
H. Encouraging experimentation
I. Appraising employee morale
J. Providing for intervisitation

II. Practices Commonly Classified as "Administrative"
A. Management of the office
B. Arrangement of schedules for extra duties
C. Assignment of rooms or areas
D. Distribution of supplies
E. Keeping records and reports
F. Care of audio-visual materials
G. Keeping inventory records
H. Checking record cards and books

I. Programming special activities
J. Checking on the attendance and punctuality of employees

III. Practices Commonly Classified as Both "Supervisory" and "Administrative"
A. Program construction
B. Testing or evaluating outcomes
C. Personnel accounting
D. Ordering instructional materials

RESPONSIBILITIES OF THE SUPERVISOR

A person employed in a supervisory capacity must constantly be able to improve his own efficiency and ability. He represent the employer to the employees and only continuous self-examination can make him a capable supervisor.

Leadership and training are the supervisor's responsibility. An efficient working unit is one in which the employees work with the supervisor. It is his job to bring out the best in his employees. He must always be relaxed, courteous, and calm in his association with his employees. Their feelings are important, and a harsh attitude does not develop the most efficient employees.

COMPETENCES OF THE SUPERVISOR

I. Complete knowledge of the duties and responsibilities of his position.
II. To be able to organize a job, plan ahead, and carry through.
III. To have self-confidence and initiative.
IV. To be able to handle the unexpected situation and make quick decisions.
V. To be able to properly train subordinates in the positions they are best suited for.
VI. To be able to keep good human relations among his subordinates.
VII. To be able to keep good human relations between his subordinates and himself and to earn their respect and trust.

THE PROFESSIONAL SUPERVISOR-EMPLOYEE RELATIONSHIP

There are two kinds of efficiency: one kind is only apparent and is produced in organizations through the exercise of mere discipline; this is but a simulation of the second, or true, efficiency which springs from spontaneous cooperation. If you are a manager, no matter how great or small your responsibility, it is your job, in the final analysis, to create and develop this involuntary cooperation among the people whom you supervise. For, no matter how powerful a combination of money, machines, and materials a company may have, this is a dead and sterile thing without a team of willing, thinking, and articulate people to guide it.

The following 21 points are presented as indicative of the exemplary basic relationship that should exist between supervisor and employee:

1. Each person wants to be liked and respected by his fellow employee and wants to be treated with consideration and respect by his superior.
2. The most competent employee will make an error. However, in a unit where good relations exist between the supervisor and his employees, tenseness and fear do not exist. Thus, errors are not hidden or covered up, and the efficiency of a unit is not impaired.

3. Subordinates resent rules, regulations, or orders that are unreasonable or unexplained.
4. Subordinates are quick to resent unfairness, harshness, injustices, and favoritism.
5. An employee will accept responsibility if he knows that he will be complimented for a job well done, and not too harshly chastised for failure; that his supervisor will check the cause of the failure, and, if it was the supervisor's fault, he will assume the blame therefore. If it was the employee's fault, his supervisor will explain the correct method or means of handling the responsibility.
6. An employee wants to receive credit for a suggestion he has made, that is used. If a suggestion cannot be used, the employee is entitled to an explanation. The supervisor should not say "no" and close the subject.
7. Fear and worry slow up a worker's ability. Poor working environment can impair his physical and mental health. A good supervisor avoids forceful methods, threats, and arguments to get a job done.
8. A forceful supervisor is able to train his employees individually and as a team, and is able to motivate them in the proper channels.
9. A mature supervisor is able to properly evaluate his subordinates and to keep them happy and satisfied.
10. A sensitive supervisor will never patronize his subordinates.
11. A worthy supervisor will respect his employees' confidences.
12. Definite and clear-cut responsibilities should be assigned to each executive.
13. Responsibility should always be coupled with corresponding authority.
14. No change should be made in the scope or responsibilities of a position without a definite understanding to that effect on the part of all persons concerned.
15. No executive or employee, occupying a single position in the organization, should be subject to definite orders from more than one source.
16. Orders should never be given to subordinates over the head of a responsible executive. Rather than do this, the officer in question should be supplanted.
17. Criticisms of subordinates should, whoever possible, be made privately, and in no case should a subordinate be criticized in the presence of executives or employees of equal or lower rank.
18. No dispute or difference between executives or employees as to authority or responsibilities should be considered too trivial for prompt and careful adjudication.
19. Promotions, wage changes, and disciplinary action should always be approved by the executive immediately superior to the one directly responsible.
20. No executive or employee should ever be required, or expected, to be at the same time an assistant to, and critic of, another.
21. Any executive whose work is subject to regular inspection should, wherever practicable, be given the assistance and facilities necessary to enable him to maintain an independent check of the quality of his work.

MINI-TEXT IN SUPERVISION, ADMINISTRATION, MANAGEMENT, AND ORGANIZATION

I. Brief Highlights

Listed concisely and sequentially are major headings and important data in the field for quick recall and review.

A. Levels of Management

Any organization of some size has several levels of management. In terms of a ladder, the levels are:

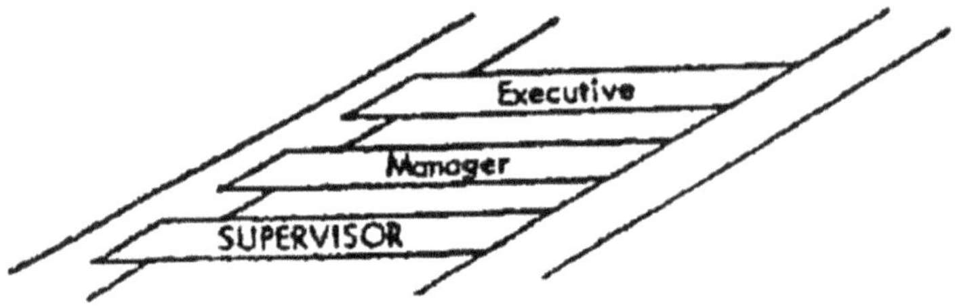

The first level is very important because it is the beginning point of management leadership.

B. What the Supervisor Must Learn

A supervisor must learn to:

1. Deal with people and their differences
2. Get the job done through people
3. Recognize the problems when they exist
4. Overcome obstacles to good performance
5. Evaluate the performance of people
6. Check his own performance in terms of accomplishment

C. A Definition of Supervisor

The term supervisor means any individual having authority, in the interests of the employer, to hire, transfer, suspend, lay-off, recall, promote, discharge, assign, reward, or discipline other employees or responsibility to direct them, or to adjust their grievances, or effectively to recommend such action, if, in connection with the foregoing, exercise of such authority is not of a merely routine or clerical nature but requires the use of independent judgment.

D. Elements of the Team Concept

What is involved in teamwork? The component parts are:

1. Members
2. A leader
3. Goals
4. Plans
5. Cooperation
6. Spirit

E. Principles of Organization

1. A team member must know what his job is.
2. Be sure that the nature and scope of a job are understood.
3. Authority and responsibility should be carefully spelled out.
4. A supervisor should be permitted to make the maximum number of decisions affecting his employees.
5. Employees should report to only one supervisor.
6. A supervisor should direct only as many employees as he can handle effectively.
7. An organization plan should be flexible.

8. Inspection and performance of work should be separate.
9. Organizational problems should receive immediate attention.
10. Assign work in line with ability and experience.

F. The Four Important Parts of Every Job
1. Inherent in every job is the *accountability* for results.
2. A second set of factors in every job is *responsibilities*.
3. Along with duties and responsibilities one must have the *authority* to act within certain limits without obtaining permission to proceed.
4. No job exists in a vacuum. The supervisor is surrounded by key *relationships*.

G. Principles of Delegation
Where work is delegated for the first time, the supervisor should think in terms of these questions:
1. Who is best qualified to do this?
2. Can an employee improve his abilities by doing this?
3. How long should an employee spend on this?
4. Are there any special problems for which he will need guidance?
5. How broad a delegation can I make?

H. Principles of Effective Communications
1. Determine the media.
2. To whom directed?
3. Identification and source authority.
4. Is communication understood?

I. Principles of Work Improvement
1. Most people usually do only the work which is assigned to them.
2. Workers are likely to fit assigned work into the time available to perform it.
3. A good workload usually stimulates output.
4. People usually do their best work when they know that results will be reviewed or inspected.
5. Employees usually feel that someone else is responsible for conditions of work, workplace layout, job methods, type of tools/equipment, and other such factors.
6. Employees are usually defensive about their job security.
7. Employees have natural resistance to change.
8. Employees can support or destroy a supervisor.
9. A supervisor usually earns the respect of his people through his personal example of diligence and efficiency.

J. Areas of Job Improvement
The areas of job improvement are quite numerous, but the most common ones which a supervisor can identify and utilize are:
1. Departmental layout
2. Flow of work
3. Workplace layout
4. Utilization of manpower
5. Work methods
6. Materials handling

7. Utilization
8. Motion economy

K. Seven Key Points in Making Improvements
1. Select the job to be improved
2. Study how it is being done now
3. Question the present method
4. Determine actions to be taken
5. Chart proposed method
6. Get approval and apply
7. Solicit worker participation

I. Corrective Techniques of Job Improvement
Specific Problems
1. Size of workload
2. Inability to meet schedules
3. Strain and fatigue
4. Improper use of men and skills
5. Waste, poor quality, unsafe conditions
6. Bottleneck conditions that hinder output
7. Poor utilization of equipment and machine
8. Efficiency and productivity of labor

General Improvement
1. Departmental layout
2. Flow of work
3. Work plan layout
4. Utilization of manpower
5. Work methods
6. Materials handling
7. Utilization of equipment
8. Motion economy

Corrective Techniques
1. Study with scale model
2. Flow chart study
3. Motion analysis
4. Comparison of units produced to standard allowance
5. Methods analysis
6. Flow chart and equipment study
7. Down time vs. running time
8. Motion analysis

M. A Planning Checklist
1. Objectives
2. Controls
3. Delegations
4. Communications
5. Resources
6. Manpower

7. Equipment
8. Supplies and materials
9. Utilization of time
10. Safety
11. Money
12. Work
13. Timing of improvements

N. Five Characteristics of Good Directions

In order to get results, directions must be:

1. Possible of accomplishment
2. Agreeable with worker interests
3. Related to mission
4. Planned and complete
5. Unmistakably clear

O. Types of Directions

1. Demands or direct orders
2. Requests
3. Suggestion or implication
4. volunteering

P. Controls

A typical listing of the overall areas in which the supervisor should establish controls might be:

1. Manpower
2. Materials
3. Quality of work
4. Quantity of work
5. Time
6. Space
7. Money
8. Methods

Q. Orienting the New Employee

1. Prepare for him
2. Welcome the new employee
3. Orientation for the job
4. Follow-up

R. Checklist for Orienting New Employees	Yes	No
1. Do you appreciate the feelings of new employees when they first report for work?	___	___
2. Are you aware of the fact that the new employee must make a big adjustment to his job?	___	___
3. Have you given him good reasons for liking the job and the organization?	___	___
4. Have you prepared for his first day on the job?	___	___
5. Did you welcome him cordially and make him feel needed?	___	___

	Yes	No
6. Did you establish rapport with him so that he feels free to talk and discuss matters with you?	___	___
7. Did you explain his job to him and his relationship to you?	___	___
8. Does he know that his work will be evaluated periodically on a basis that is fair and objective?	___	___
9. Did you introduce him to his fellow workers in such a way that they are likely to accept him?	___	___
10. Does he know what employee benefits he will receive?	___	___
11. Does he understand the importance of being on the job and what to do if he must leave his duty station?	___	___
12. Has he been impressed with the importance of accident prevention and safe practice?	___	___
13. Does he generally know his way around the department?	___	___
14. Is he under the guidance of a sponsor who will teach the right way of doing things?	___	___
15. Do you plan to follow-up so that he will continue to adjust successfully to his job?	___	___

S. Principles of Learning
1. Motivation
2. Demonstration or explanation
3. Practice

T. Causes of Poor Performance
1. Improper training for job
2. Wrong tools
3. Inadequate directions
4. Lack of supervisory follow-up
5. Poor communications
6. Lack of standards of performance
7. Wrong work habits
8. Low morale
9. Other

U. Four Major Steps in On-The-Job Instruction
1. Prepare the worker
2. Present the operation
3. Tryout performance
4. Follow-up

V. Employees Want Five Things
1. Security
2. Opportunity
3. Recognition
4. Inclusion
5. Expression

W. Some Don'ts in Regard to Praise
1. Don't praise a person for something he hasn't done.
2. Don't praise a person unless you can be sincere.
3. Don't be sparing in praise just because your superior withholds it from you.
4. Don't let too much time elapse between good performance and recognition of it

X. How to Gain Your Workers' Confidence
Methods of developing confidence include such things as:
1. Knowing the interests, habits, hobbies of employees
2. Admitting your own inadequacies
3. Sharing and telling of confidence in others
4. Supporting people when they are in trouble
5. Delegating matters that can be well handled
6. Being frank and straightforward about problems and working conditions
7. Encouraging others to bring their problems to you
8. Taking action on problems which impede worker progress

Y. Sources of Employee Problems
On-the-job causes might be such things as:
1. A feeling that favoritism is exercised in assignments
2. Assignment of overtime
3. An undue amount of supervision
4. Changing methods or systems
5. Stealing of ideas or trade secrets
6. Lack of interest in job
7. Threat of reduction in force
8. Ignorance or lack of communications
9. Poor equipment
10. Lack of knowing how supervisor feels toward employee
11. Shift assignments

Off-the-job problems might have to do with:
1. Health
2. Finances
3. Housing
4. Family

Z. The Supervisor's Key to Discipline
There are several key points about discipline which the supervisor should keep in mind:
1. Job discipline is one of the disciplines of life and is directed by the supervisor.
2. It is more important to correct an employee fault than to fix blame for it.
3. Employee performance is affected by problems both on the job and off.
4. Sudden or abrupt changes in behavior can be indications of important employee problems.
5. Problems should be dealt with as soon as possible after they are identified.
6. The attitude of the supervisor may have more to do with solving problems than the techniques of problem solving.
7. Correction of employee behavior should be resorted to only after the supervisor is sure that training or counseling will not be helpful.

8. Be sure to document your disciplinary actions.
9. Make sure that you are disciplining on the basis of facts rather than personal feelings.
10. Take each disciplinary step in order, being careful not to make snap judgments, or decisions based on impatience.

AA. Five Important Processes of Management
1. Planning
2. Organizing
3. Scheduling
4. Controlling
5. Motivating

BB. When the Supervisor Fails to Plan
1. Supervisor creates impression of not knowing his job
2. May lead to excessive overtime
3. Job runs itself—supervisor lacks control
4. Deadlines and appointments missed
5. Parts of the work go undone
6. Work interrupted by emergencies
7. Sets a bad example
8. Uneven workload creates peaks and valleys
9. Too much time on minor details at expense of more important tasks

CC. Fourteen General Principles of Management
1. Division of work
2. Authority and responsibility
3. Discipline
4. Unity of command
5. Unity of direction
6. Subordination of individual interest to general interest
7. Remuneration of personnel
8. Centralization
9. Scalar chain
10. Order
11. Equity
12. Stability of tenure of personnel
13. Initiative
14. Esprit de corps

DD. Change

Bringing about change is perhaps attempted more often, and yet less well understood, than anything else the supervisor does. How do people generally react to change? (People tend to resist change that is imposed upon them by other individuals or circumstances.

Change is characteristic of every situation. It is a part of every real endeavor where the efforts of people are concerned.

1. Why do people resist change?
   People may resist change because of:
   a. Fear of the unknown
   b. Implied criticism
   c. Unpleasant experiences in the past
   d. Fear of loss of status
   e. Threat to the ego
   f. Fear of loss of economic stability

2. How can we best overcome the resistance to change?
   In initiating change, take these steps:
   a. Get ready to sell
   b. Identify sources of help
   c. Anticipate objections
   d. Sell benefits
   e. Listen in depth
   f. Follow up

II. Brief Topical Summaries

A. Who/What is the Supervisor?
   1. The supervisor is often called the "highest level employee and the lowest level manager."
   2. A supervisor is a member of both management and the work group. He acts as a bridge between the two.
   3. Most problems in supervision are in the area of human relations, or people problems.
   4. Employees expect: Respect, opportunity to learn and to advance, and a sense of belonging, and so forth.
   5. Supervisors are responsible for directing people and organizing work. Planning is of paramount importance.
   6. A position description is a set of duties and responsibilities inherent to a given position.
   7. It is important to keep the position description up-to-date and to provide each employee with his own copy.

B. The Sociology of Work
   1. People are alike in many ways; however, each individual is unique.
   2. The supervisor is challenged in getting to know employee differences. Acquiring skills in evaluating individuals is an asset.
   3. Maintaining meaningful working relationships in the organization is of great importance.
   4. The supervisor has an obligation to help individuals to develop to their fullest potential.
   5. Job rotation on a planned basis helps to build versatility and to maintain interest and enthusiasm in work groups.
   6. Cross training (job rotation) provides backup skills.

7. The supervisor can help reduce tension by maintaining a sense of humor, providing guidance to employees, and by making reasonable and timely decisions. Employees respond favorably to working under reasonably predictable circumstances.
8. Change is characteristic of all managerial behavior. The supervisor must adjust to changes in procedures, new methods, technological changes, and to a number of new and sometimes challenging situations.
9. To overcome the natural tendency for people to resist change, the supervisor should become more skillful in initiating change.

C. Principles and Practices of Supervision

1. Employees should be required to answer to only one superior.
2. A supervisor can effectively direct only a limited number of employees, depending upon the complexity, variety, and proximity of the jobs involved.
3. The organizational chart presents the organization in graphic form. It reflects lines of authority and responsibility as well as interrelationships of units within the organization.
4. Distribution of work can be improved through an analysis using the "Work Distribution Chart."
5. The "Work Distribution Chart" reflects the division of work within a unit in understandable form.
6. When related tasks are given to an employee, he has a better chance of increasing his skills through training.
7. The individual who is given the responsibility for tasks must also be given the appropriate authority to insure adequate results.
8. The supervisor should delegate repetitive, routine work. Preparation of recurring reports, maintaining leave and attendance records are some examples.
9. Good discipline is essential to good task performance. Discipline is reflected in the actions of employees on the job in the absence of supervision.
10. Disciplinary action may have to be taken when the positive aspects of discipline have failed. Reprimand, warning, and suspension are examples of disciplinary action.
11. If a situation calls for a reprimand, be sure it is deserved and remember it is to be done in private.

D. Dynamic Leadership

1. A style is a personal method or manner of exerting influence.
2. Authoritarian leaders often see themselves as the source of power and authority.
3. The democratic leader often perceives the group as the source of authority and power.
4. Supervisors tend to do better when using the pattern of leadership that is most natural for them.
5. Social scientists suggest that the effective supervisor use the leadership style that best fits the problem or circumstances involved.
6. All four styles—telling, selling, consulting, joining—have their place. Using one does not preclude using the other at another time.

7. The theory X point of view assumes that the average person dislikes work, will avoid it whenever possible, and must be coerced to achieve organizational objectives.
8. The theory Y point of view assumes that the average person considers work to be a natural as play, and, when the individual is committed, he requires little supervision or direction to accomplish desired objectives.
9. The leader's basic assumptions concerning human behavior and human nature affect his actions, decisions, and other managerial practices.
10. Dissatisfaction among employees is often present, but difficult to isolate. The supervisor should seek to weaken dissatisfaction by keeping promises, being sincere and considerate, keeping employees informed, and so forth.
11. Constructive suggestions should be encouraged during the natural progress of the work.

E. Processes for Solving Problems

1. People find their daily tasks more meaningful and satisfying when they can improve them.
2. The causes of problems, or the key factors, are often hidden in the background. Ability to solve problems often involves the ability to isolate them from their backgrounds. There is some substance to the cliché that some persons "can't see the forest for the trees."
3. New procedures are often developed from old ones. Problems should be broken down into manageable parts. New ideas can be adapted from old one.
4. People think differently in problem-solving situations. Using a logical, patterned approach is often useful. One approach found to be useful includes these steps:
   a. Define the problem
   b. Establish objectives
   c. Get the facts
   d. Weigh and decide
   e. Take action
   f. Evaluate action

F. Training for Results

1. Participants respond best when they feel training is important to them.
2. The supervisor has responsibility for the training and development of those who report to him.
3. When training is delegated to others, great care must be exercised to insure the trainer has knowledge, aptitude, and interest for his work as a trainer.
4. Training (learning) of some type goes on continually. The most successful supervisor makes certain the learning contributes in a productive manner to operational goals.
5. New employees are particularly susceptible to training. Older employees facing new job situations require specific training, as well as having need for development and growth opportunities.
6. Training needs require continuous monitoring.
7. The training officer of an agency is a professional with a responsibility to assist supervisors in solving training problems.

8. Many of the self-development steps important to the supervisor's own growth are equally important to the development of peers and subordinates. Knowledge of these is important when the supervisor consults with others on development and growth opportunities.

G. Health, Safety, and Accident Prevention

1. Management-minded supervisors take appropriate measures to assist employees in maintaining health and in assuring safe practices in the work environment.
2. Effective safety training and practices help to avoid injury and accidents.
3. Safety should be a management goal. All infractions of safety which are observed should be corrected without exception.
4. Employees' safety attitude, training and instruction, provision of safe tools and equipment, supervision, and leadership are considered highly important factors which contribute to safety and which can be influenced directly by supervisors.
5. When accidents do occur, they should be investigated promptly for very important reasons, including the fact that information which is gained can be used to prevent accidents in the future.

H. Equal Employment Opportunity

1. The supervisor should endeavor to treat all employees fairly, without regard to religion, race, sex, or national origin.
2. Groups tend to reflect the attitude of the leader. Prejudice can be detected even in very subtle form. Supervisors must strive to create a feeling of mutual respect and confidence in every employee.
3. Complete utilization of all human resources is a national goal. Equitable consideration should be accorded women in the work force, minority-group members, the physically and mentally handicapped, and the older employee. The important question is: "Who can do the job?"
4. Training opportunities, recognition for performance, overtime assignments, promotional opportunities, and all other personnel actions are to be handled on an equitable basis.

I. Improving Communications

1. Communications is achieving understanding between the sender and the receiver of a message. It also means sharing information—the creation of understanding.
2. Communication is basic to all human activity. Words are means of conveying meanings; however, real meanings are in people.
3. There are very practical differences in the effectiveness of one-way, impersonal, and two-way communications. Words spoken face-to-face are better understood. Telephone conversations are effective, but lack the rapport of person-to-person exchanges. The whole person communicates.
4. Cooperation and communication in an organization go hand in hand. When there is a mutual respect between people, spelling out rules and procedures for communicating is unnecessary.
5. There are several barriers to effective communications. These include failure to listen with respect and understanding, lack of skill in feedback, and misinterpreting the meanings of words used by the speaker. It is also common

practice to listen to what we want to hear, and tune out things we do not want to hear.

6. Communication is management's chief problem. The supervisor should accept the challenge to communicate more effectively and to improve interagency and intra-agency communications.
7. The supervisor may often plan for and conduct meetings. The planning phase is critical and may determine the success or the failure of a meeting.
8. Speaking before groups usually requires extra effort. Stage fright may never disappear completely, but it can be controlled.

J. Self-Development

1. Every employee is responsible for his own self-development.
2. Toastmaster and toastmistress clubs offer opportunities to improve skills in oral communications.
3. Planning for one's own self-development is of vital importance. Supervisors know their own strengths and limitations better than anyone else.
4. Many opportunities are open to aid the supervisor in his developmental efforts, including job assignments; training opportunities, both governmental and non-governmental—to include universities and professional conferences and seminars.
5. Programmed instruction offers a means of studying at one's own rate.
6. Where difficulties may arise from a supervisor's being away from his work for training, he may participate in televised home study or correspondence courses to meet his self-development needs.

K. Teaching and Training

1. The Teaching Process

   Teaching is encouraging and guiding the learning activities of students toward established goals. In most cases this process consists of five steps: preparation, presentation, summarization, evaluation, and application.

   a. Preparation

      Preparation is two-fold in nature; that of the supervisor and the employee. Preparation by the supervisor is absolutely essential to success. He must know what, when, where, how, and whom he will teach. Some of the factors that should be considered are:

      1) The objectives
      2) The materials needed
      3) The methods to be used
      4) Employee participation
      5) Employee interest
      6) Training aids
      7) Evaluation
      8) Summarization

      Employee preparation consists in preparing the employee to receive the material. Probably the most important single factor in the preparation of the employee is arousing and maintaining his interest. He must know the objectives of the training, why he is there, how the material can be used, and its importance to him.

b. Presentation
In presentation, have a carefully designed plan and follow it. The plan should be accurate and complete, yet flexible enough to meet situations as they arise. The method of presentation will be determined by the particular situation and objectives.

c. Summary
A summary should be made at the end of every training unit and program. In addition, there may be internal summaries depending on the nature of the material being taught. The important thing is that the trainee must always be able to understand how each part of the new material relates to the whole.

d. Application
The supervisor must arrange work so the employee will be given a chance to apply new knowledge or skills while the material is still clear in his mind and interest is high. The trainee does not really know whether he has learned the material until he has been given a chance to apply it. If the material is not applied, it loses most of its value.

e. Evaluation
The purpose of all training is to promote learning. To determine whether the training has been a success or failure, the supervisor must evaluate this learning.
In the broadest sense, evaluation includes all the devices, methods, skills, and techniques used by the supervisor to keep himself and the employees informed as to their progress toward the objectives they are pursuing. The extent to which the employee has mastered the knowledge, skills, and abilities, or changed his attitudes, as determined by the program objectives, is the extent to which instruction has succeeded or failed.
Evaluation should not be confined to the end of the lesson, day, or program but should be used continuously. We shall note later the way this relates to the rest of the teaching process.

2. Teaching Methods
A teaching method is a pattern of identifiable student and instructor activity used in presenting training material.
All supervisors are faced with the problem of deciding which method should be used at a given time.

a. Lecture
The lecture is direct oral presentation of material by the supervisor. The present trend is to place less emphasis on the trainer's activity and more on that of the trainee.

b. Discussion
Teaching by discussion or conference involves using questions and other techniques to arouse interest and focus attention upon certain areas, and by doing so creating a learning situation. This can be one of the most

valuable methods because it gives the employees an opportunity to express their ideas and pool their knowledge.

c. Demonstration
The demonstration is used to teach how something works or how to do something. It can be used to show a principle or what the results of a series of actions will be. A well-staged demonstration is particularly effective because it shows proper methods of performance in a realistic manner.

d. Performance
Performance is one of the most fundamental of all learning techniques or teaching methods. The trainee may be able to tell how a specific operation should be performed but he cannot be sure he knows how to perform the operation until he has done so.
As with all methods, there are certain advantages and disadvantages to each method.

e. Which Method to Use
Moreover, there are other methods and techniques of teaching. It is difficult to use any method without other methods entering into it. In any learning situation, a combination of methods is usually more effective than any one method alone.

Finally, evaluation must be integrated into the other aspects of the teaching-learning process.

It must be used in the motivation of the trainees; it must be used to assist in developing understanding during the training; and it must be related to employee application of the results of training.

This is distinctly the role of the supervisor.

SCHOOL BUS OPERATIONS

SPECIAL EDUCATION OPERATION

NATIONAL MINIMUM STANDARD GUIDELINES FOR SCHOOL BUS OPERATIONS

INTRODUCTION TO OPERATIONS

A successful school transportation operation depends upon a high quality of dedication and performance by all those who are associated with it. This includes the school administrator, transportation director, supervisor, contractor, vehicle maintenance and service personnel, teachers, passengers, the public, and, most importantly, the driver of the school bus.

As school transportation operations expand, the driving environment becomes more complex. Also, inflation escalates the cost of vehicles and repairs and fuel becomes less available and/or more expensive. Therefore, school administrators must meet the challange to maintain increasingly high standards of safety and performance for all elements of the school transportation systems.

SCHOOL BUS OPERATIONS

I. ADMINISTRATION

A. The state agency(ies) responsible for pupil transportation should provide the following:

1. Leadership in the development of a comprehensive pupil transportation program for state-wide application.
2. A State Director of pupil transporation with the staff and other resources required to optimally perform the job.
3. A clear, concise pupil transportation policy.
4. A cost accounting system for all expenditures in the area of pupil transportation.
5. A state-wide management information system to accommodate pupil transportation data, i.e., costs, accidents and injuries, manpower availability, etc.
6. A promotion of pupil transportation safety program utilizing community, legislature, media, law-enforcement agencies and other state agencies concerned with pupil transportation.
7. A manual or handbook for local pupil transporation supervisors and school administrators containing detailed instructions for implementing the state's pupil transportation policies.
8. A manual or handbook for each school bus driver containing the state pupil transportation regulations.
9. A comprehensive school bus driver training program for both pre-service and inservice instruction.
10. A manual or handbook for school bus maintenance personnel.
11. Workshops, seminars and/or conferences for all pupil transportation personnel.
12. Encouragement for institutions of higher learning throughout the state to provide undergraduate and graduate courses in pupil transportation operation and safety. Instruction should be acceptable for certification purposes.
13. Safety and ridership curricula for pupil passengers.
14. Annual visits to local school systems to evaluate transportation systems and provide direction as necessary.
15. Bus and equipment standards that would be conducive to better and safer bus performance.

16. Coordination with other agencies having responsibility for pupil transportation services.

B. Local Administrators should:

1. Implement the state pupil transportation policy.
2. Become involved in the pupil transportation operation within their jurisdiction, including participation in training programs for all transportational personnel; review of school bus routes; provisions for supervision of loading and unloading areas at or near the school; investigation and reporting of accidents and other transportation problems and evaluation of the pupil transportation system. (Suggested action to be taken during and following observation of a school bus route appears at Appendix A.)
3. Provide resource material and require teachers to include instruction in passenger safety in the school curriculum, in compliance with Federal Standard 17.
4. Provide close continuous supervision of loading and unloading areas at or near the school and emergency evacuation drills.
5. Provide adequate supervision for pupils whose bus schedules require them to arrive at school before classes begin and/or remain after classes terminate.
6. Promote public understanding of, and support for, the school system's transportation program.
7. Develop local pupil transportation policies and regulations, including special education transportation policies.

II. PUPIL TRANSPORTATION DIRECTOR

A. State Pupil Transportation Director:

1. Specific duties include, but are not limited to:
   a. Assist in implementing basic pupil transportation policies throughout the state.
   b. Manage the state's pupil transportation program. This includes the ability to plan and budget for the operation and to forecast requirements.
   c. Supervise the preparation of manuals or handbooks for local transportation personnel, and for school bus contractors.
   d. Provide assistance to local school administrators upon request, and direction as may be necessary.

e. Assist in evaluation of state and local operations and provide recommendations when appropriate.

f. Plan and direct training for pupil transportation personnel.

g. Assist local personnel in planning and conducting workshops for pupil passenger safety.

h. Require and maintain appropriate reports and records.

B. Local Pupil Transportation Director and/or Private Operator:

1. Specific duties include, but are not limited to:

a. Provide assistance in planning, budgeting, and forecasting for the pupil transportation system.

b. Assist school officials in school site selection and plant planning.

c. Provide for chassis and body procurement when appropriate.

d. Develop and implement a plan for maintenance of equipment.

e. Recruit, select, instruct, and supervise personnel.

f. Route and schedule buses.

g. Assist in the development and implementation of safety instructional programs for pupils.

h. Work with administrators, teachers, transportation personnel, students, parents, and various public and private agencies to improve the quality of the transportation system.

i. Investigate and report accidents and other problems associated with the pupil transportation system.

j. Keep records and prepare reports.

k. Develop and supervise the implementation of an ongoing evaluation plan for the pupil transportation system.

2. The pupil transportation director and/or private operator should have an understanding of the educational process and the role of transportation in this process. Qualifications should include:

a. A satisfactory driving record as revealed through checks with the National Driver Register Service and the State Department of Motor Vehicles.

b. A satisfactory work history and a record free of criminal convictions. (The same type of checks should be made of the applicant who seeks employment as a driver of a school bus.) Suggestions as to how this information may be obtained appear in Section III.

c. An undergraduate degree or equivalent experience in one or more of the following major fields of study: education, business administration, management, transportation, or a related field.

d. The ability to work effectively with a broad range of individuals and organizations.

e. The ability to manage personnel and resources to achieve a desired objective.

3. The school transportation director and/or private operator should receive formal instruction in pupil transportation management. This training should include classroom work and field experience.

III. DRIVER

A. There are certain duties that all school bus drivers are required to perform. These may include:

1. Safe and efficient operation of the vehicle.

2. Conduct thorough pre-trip and post-trip checks on the vehicle and its special equipment.

3. Maintain orderly conduct of passengers.

4. Meet emergency situations in accordance with operating procedures.

5. Communicate effectively with school staff and public.

6. Complete required reports.

7. Successfully complete training programs.

8. Provide maximum safety for passengers while on the bus and during loading and unloading.

9. Wearing seat belt when bus is in operation.

B. Procedures for selecting school bus drivers should include:

1. A proper application form on which information of a personal and occupational history is requested. (An example of a form that the school district may want to use to seek personal and work history information appears at Appendix B.)

2. A check of applicant's driving record. (Checks of the National

Driver Register and of the files of the State Department of Motor Vehicles are considered essential in the case of the individual who is applying for a position as a school bus driver.)

NOTE: The applicant should be told that these checks will be made before being asked to complete the application for employment. Establish criteria for rejection of persons with unacceptable driving records.

3. A check to determine if an applicant has a record of criminal convictions. Establish criteria for rejecting those with unacceptable convictions.

4. One or more personal interviews. (A properly conducted interview can be one of the most important of the selection procedures.)

5. A physical examination administered by a School Board approved licensed physician. Tests for TB and other communicable diseases should be included. The physical examination should be conducted annually and at such other times as the school superintendent may deem necessary. (An example appears in Appendix C.)

6. A determination of educational attainment. An applicant for position as a school bus driver should demonstrate the ability to follow detailed written instructions and the ability to record and report data accurately.

C. Instructional Program for School Bus Drivers:

1. Adequate classroom and behind-the-wheel training in a state approved pre-service training program that enables the applicant to handle the vehicle in a safe and efficient manner prior to transporting pupils shall be required.

2. Annual state approved in-service training program shall be required.

D. Each state should develop and make available to each school bus driver a driver's manual or handbook at the time of hiring. (see Section I). This manual should include the following subjects:

1. The transportation policy of the school system.

2. Motor vehicle rules and regulations applicable to school bus operation.

3. Vehicle operation and maintenance.

4. Procedure following involvement in, or approaching, a highway crash.

5. Rudiments of basic first aid procedures. Local school systems should supplement the state-produced manual with information on local policy and practices that may vary from, but should not

conflict with, state level requirements.

E. Behind-the-wheel instruction should be given in the same type and size bus the driver will be operating. When the driver will be expected to operate more than one size and type of vehicle, instruction should be given in the specific handling characteristics of each different vehicle. This instruction should include:

1. Familiarization with the bus and its equipment.
2. Emergency exit drills. (see Appendix D)
3. Use of the special warning and stop lamps and other traffic control devices.
4. Procedures for loading and unloading pupils at bus stops.
5. The necessity for cooperating with other highway users.
6. Entrance to and departure from loading and unloading areas at school buildings.
7. Entrance to and departure from the bus garage or other storage area.
8. Procedure for reporting mechanical difficulties.
9. Post-accident and post-road failure procedures.
10. Procedure for performing pre-trip and post-trip inspections.
11. Procedure for recognizing cause and effect relationship between driving habits and vehicle maintenance.

F. School bus drivers should be evaluated at regular intervals. These evaluations may include:

1. Written tests.
2. Road performance check.
3. Evaluation interviews.

IV. **BUS AIDE:** (See Special Education Section)

V. **MAINTENANCE AND SERVICE PERSONNEL**

A. Adequate staff should be employed to perform maintenance functions on a timely basis consistent with safe transportation practices.

B. Instructional Program for Maintenance and Service Personnel.

1. The transportation system should develop and make available to

maintenance and service personnel the required maintenance and service publications for the equipment being serviced.

2. The transportation system should arrange for pre-service and in-service training for maintenance and service personnel at regular intervals. They should also require or encourage maintenance personnel to attend state-sponsored workshops or training institutes. The training program should include instruction in:

   a. Preventive maintenance procedures.

   b. Repair procedures for each type of vehicle in the fleet and its special equipment.

   c. Service procedures for equipment.

   d. Inspection of the vehicle and its equipment.

   e. Recovery procedures for vehicles involved in an accident or breakdown.

   f. Preparation of maintenance records.

   g. A planned parts and equipment stock.

   h. Establishment of parts inventory control procedures.

VI. PUPIL MANAGEMENT

The program for pupil management should be developed cooperatively by responsible school administrators and transportation personnel. The program should be designed to insure the safety and welfare of all school bus passengers.

A. Policies should include but not be limited to:

   1. The bus driver's authority over, and responsibility for, pupils while in transit.

   2. The pupil's right to "due process" when disciplinary action is taken.

   3. The procedure for resolving problems when the driver needs assistance.

   4. The conditions under which a pupil might be temporarily suspended from the privilege of riding the bus.

   5. Procedures for handling emergencies.

   6. Use of bus monitors (or driver aides).

   7. Requirements and responsibility for school bus passenger and

pedestrian safety instruction.

8. Parental responsibility for damage to bus and/or equipment by their children.

B. Pupil Regulations:

Each school system should have a written set of regulations for transported pupils. These regulations should set forth standards of behavior and promote orderly conduct necessary for safe and efficient transportation. Regulations should include but may not be limited to:

1. Pupil shall arrive at the bus stop before the bus arrives.
2. Wait in a safe place, clear of traffic and away from where the bus stops.
3. Wait in an orderly line and avoid "horseplay."
4. Go directly to an available, or assigned seat when entering the bus.
5. Remain seated, keep aisles and exits clear.
6. Observe classroom conduct, and obey the driver promptly and respectfully.
7. Prohibit the use of profane language, eating and drinking of any type on the bus.
8. Prohibit the use of tobacco, alcohol or drugs and controlled substances.
9. Prohibit the throwing or passing of objects on, from or into buses.
10. Permit pupils to carry only objects that can be held on their laps.
11. Prohibit hazardous materials, objects and animals on the bus.
12. Respect the rights and safety of others.
13. Prohibit leaving or boarding the bus at locations other than the assigned home stop or assigned school.
14. Prohibit putting head, arms or objects out of bus windows.
15. Prohibit hooky-bobbing (hitching rides via rear bumper).

C. Behavior Control:

Proper pupil behavior is important. The distraction of the driver can contribute to accidents. Pupils and parents should be made aware of and abide by reasonable regulations to enhance safety. The consequences of unacceptable behavior should be clearly understood. The following procedures will protect the pupil's rights and maintain order on the bus:

1. The bus driver should establish proper rapport.
2. The bus driver should handle minor infractions through discussion with pupils and/or assignment of seats. (Sometimes a call to the parents will improve behavior.)
3. In case of serious or recurring misconduct, the bus driver must describe the violations in writing on the appropriate forms to the person designated to deal with discipline.
4. First offenses require at least a notification to the pupil and parent(s) either by phone or in person. Second or subsequent offenses may require a conference with the pupil, parents, driver, and school administrator(s) and could result in some period of suspension of pupil's riding privileges.
5. Suspend pupil's riding privileges when the safe operation of the bus is jeopardized.

D. Instruction:

Most pupils ride school buses to and from school or on activity trips. It is important that all pupils be taught safe riding and pedestrian practices. This instruction should be given as soon as practical at the beginning of the school year. Appropriate instruction should be developed for each grade level and should include:

1. Safe walking practices to and from the bus stop.
2. Wearing of light-colored or reflective clothing when going to and from bus stop in darkness.
3. How and where to wait safely for the bus.
4. What to do if the bus is late, or does not arrive.
5. How to enter and leave the bus. (use hand rail, etc.)
6. Safe riding practices.
7. Procedures for emergency evacuation. (See appendix D)
8. Safely crossing the highway before boarding and after leaving the bus.
9. Procedures to follow in emergencies.
10. Proper respect for the rights and privileges of others.

VII. PROCEDURES

A. Policy. The responsible state agency and the local school system should have clear and concise policies concerning the conditions for the operation of contractor and/or public-owned school buses within local school systems. Following are examples of the subjects that should be treated in the policy document:

1. Procedure for determining eligibility for pupil transportation service.

2. Procurement of equipment and supplies, maintenance and inspection procedures, and time period over which equipment will be depreciated.

3. Driver recruitment, selection, instruction, placement, and supervision.

4. Determination of areas in which the school will provide transportation services.

5. Principles of routing, establishing stops, and scheduling buses.

6. Use of special lighting and signaling equipment on school buses.

   a. Alternately flashing signal lamps shall be used when the bus is stopping or stopped for the purpose of taking on or discharging passengers, as follows:

      (1) Alternately flashing amber lamps are to be used to warn motorists that the bus is stopping to take on or to discharge passengers.

      (2) Alternately flashing red lights are to be used to inform motorists that the bus is stopped on the roadway to take on or discharge passengers.

   b. When a stop arm is used, it shall be operated simultaneously with the flashing red signal lamps.

   c. A white flashing strobe light may be used to increase the visibility of the school bus on the highway during adverse visibility conditions.

7. Policy with regard to standees, the length of time in transit and the type of supervision to be provided while pupils are on the bus and at school prior to the beginning and following the end of classes.

   a. Each occupant shall be properly seated and no standees will be permitted while the bus is in motion.

8. Policy with regard to the transportation of non-public school pupils.

    a. Such policy shall be determined by State statute and/or State regulations.

9. Policy relative to the supervision of pupils while loading and unloading at school sites and while enroute.

    a. Local school districts shall be responsible for such policy development.

10. Procedure to be observed in the employment of adult monitors to supervise the loading, transportation, and unloading of pupils requiring special care.

11. Procedure for evaluating the school transportation system and how frequently this should be done.

B. School Site Selection and Plant Planning. When school sites are being selected, consideration should be given to the safety of pupils riding school buses. School buses will be required to utilize the roads in and around the school site, plus public roadways leading into and from the school area. High density traffic flow near school exits and entrances should be avoided. Proper site selection and plant planning for improved school transportation is extremely important. (See Appendix E) More specifically, school officials should provide:

1. Separate and adequate space for school bus loading zones.

2. Clearly marked and controlled walkways through school bus zones.

3. Traffic flow and parking patterns separate from the boarding area.

4. A separate loading area for wheelchairs.

5. An organized schedule of loading areas with stops clearly marked.

6. A loading and unloading site to eliminate the backing of transportation equipment.

See Appendix F, which may be used to evaluate school bus driveways in the vicinity of the school.

C. Routing and Scheduling. It is necessary to procure a map of the area served by a particular school or school system in order to establish bus routes that will adequately meet the needs of pupils in a particular area. Information on road conditions, railroad crossings, and other factors that might affect the particular operation should be recorded along with the location of homes and the number of school age children in each. (Recommended procedures for school bus drivers at railroad crossings appear in Appendix G.) Satisfactory school bus stops must be identified along streets and highways where buses can travel with the least amount of risk. The number of pupils to be transported and the distance to be traveled are primary factors in allocating equipment for a particular area. Pupils should be assigned to specific stops according to walking distances, grade level, and the school attended. Special attention must be given to the handicapped: there are a number of possible approaches to laying out school bus routes. Five routing techniques are among the most frequently used. They emphasize the necessity for pupil safety program efficiency, and operational economy.

1. Shoestring Routes. The shoestring route holds the number of miles a pupil must ride to a minimum and is the most economical if the driver lives in the vicinity of the first pupil pick-up and works in or near the attendance center during the day.

2. Circular Routes. "Circular" routes enable the first pupil who boards the bus in the morning to be the first one to disembark in the evening.

3. Retracing Routes. Retracing routes should be avoided, except when pupils would be subjected to greater than ordinary risk crossing the road after alighting from the bus. In these instances, retracing will eliminate the need for the pupil to cross the roadway.

4. Double Routing. Double routing permits one bus to transport more than one load of pupils, but requires careful planning, including school scheduling.

5. Emergency Routes. Emergency routing should be established in all school systems. When weather or road conditions dictate that it is not safe to travel on other than hard-surfaced roads, an announcement can be made by radio or other means that such routings will be used on that particular day or days.

A survey should be conducted by the pupil transportation director for the purpose of identifying factors that might indicate a route change. After the survey is completed a time study should be made by driving over the route in the same equipment that will be used in the actual operation. The driver(s) who will operate over the route(s) should regard the trip as a "dry run." All scheduled stops should be made "live" and "dead" mileage should be recorded; distance and time between stops should be indicated, etc. These data, if obtained accurately, will permit the development of a schedule which probably will need little revision once it is placed into effect. After the route has been definitely established, a schedule showing individual stops should be available in the bus for the information of substitute drivers.

Each request for new or additional service should be investigated thoroughly before making a change. This investigation often reveals characteristics about the area that would make a change in service unsatisfactory until certain conditions were corrected. It should be remembered that a stopped school bus presents a hazard when operating on thoroughfares where relatively high speeds or high traffic volume prevail. It is usually unwise for buses to take on or discharge passengers on main arteries.

Each stop should be established only after thorough investigation has revealed the location to be the most desirable in the area. It is considered poor practice to negotiate a "U turn" on main arteries of traffic even though provisions may have been made for such turns. The projection of the rear end of the bus into inside traffic lanes from medians that are too narrow to accommodate its length often create traffic interference that places the lives of transported pupils in jeopardy. Further, it is desirable to eliminate, insofar as possible, the necessity to turn the bus by backing. Bus stops should be located at a distance from the crest of a hill or curve to allow motorists traveling at the posted speed to stop within the sight distance. Additional precautions should include but may not be limited to the following:

a. Determine the location and destination of all pupils to be transported.

b. Provide the driver, the school of attendance, and the transportation office with the following information:

   (1) list of pupils on the bus(es).

   (2) approximate times for pick up and return of pupils.

   (3) map indicating routing of the bus and pupil locations.

c. Provide the parents or guardians of all pupils with the driver's name, bus number, pick up and return times, school closing information, school calendar, etc.

d. Determine the advisability of utilizing the concept of computerized scheduling.

e. Plan bus routes that will permit optimum pupil safety, program efficiency and operational economy.

D. Inspection of Equipment. A thorough and systematic inspection procedure is the essence of a planned preventive maintenance program. Daily routine inspection will alert the driver to the need for minor repairs and adjustments. Failure to conduct such inspections for any sustained period of time could result in more extensive repairs at a later date. Inspection, therefore, is an indispensable factor in a safe school transportation system.

The school bus driver is the key to an effective daily inspection program. It is the driver's responsibility to make a planned and systematic inspection of the bus before each trip. A recommended procedure requires the conducting of both stationary and operating inspections. The following outline is not suggested as a model for use but is included as a guide for transportation personnel to use in developing a systematic inspection procedure.

1. Stationary Inspection

   a. Pre-starting inspection:

      (1) Observe the bus for evidence of oil, fuel, or water leaks, vandalism, etc.

      (2) Raise the hood and make sure the safety latch or hinge is in hold position, then check oil, water, belts, hoses, and wiring for frayed, cracked and/or deteriorated conditions.

   b. Walk-around inspection:

      Place the transmission in neutral and set the parking brake (fully depress the clutch pedal in manual transmission equipped vehicles). Start the engine and inspect the bus from top to bottom and end to end. Check for:

      (1) Tires: underinflated, flat, excessive wear or damaged.

      (2) Wheels: loose or missing nuts, excessive corrosion, cracks, or other damage.

      (3) Fluid leaks: evidence of wetness on inner wheels and tires.

      (4) Windshield and driver's side window: all school bus windows should be clean.

      (5) Mirrors: adequate view to the rear is essential for safety. They must be clean, properly aimed, and tightly adjusted.

      (6) Warning systems: running lights, back-up lights, all signals and signs, reflectors, turn signals, stop lights and warning flashers must be clean and working properly.

      (7) Exhaust system: sagging exhaust pipes, short and leaky tailpipes, and defective mufflers must be repaired and replaced.

      (8) Emergency exits: must be tightly sealed to prevent possible entrance of dangerous carbon monoxide fumes. (Check by opening and closing to keep hinges operational and to check functioning of warning buzzer.)

c. Inside safety check:

(1) The passenger compartment, seats, frames, emergency exits, and windows must be carefully checked.

(2) Inspect instruments and controls. With the engine operating, check the following:

(a) Vacuum or air pressure gauge or hydraulic indicator lights: these should indicate adequate capacity to operate brakes. Loss of air or hydraulic pressure or vacuum indicates a braking deficiency that must be corrected immediately.

(b) Oil pressure gauge: the engine should be turned off in the event of inadequate pressure and reported immediately.

(c) Warning lights:

1. Oil pressure warning light: prolonged displaying of the warning light is a signal of oil pressure problems and should be reported immediately.

2. Service brake warning light: a light on during the braking application indicates that the brake system is not operating properly.

3. Alternator/Generator warning light: a continuous light "on" after the engine is running indicates a malfunction in the charging system.

4. Ammeter and/or voltmeter: any continuous discharge should be reported immediately.

5. Water temperature gauge or warning light: the indicator should always read "cool" or "warm." If it indicates "hot" the engine should be stopped immediately. The same action should be taken if the temperature warning light goes "on."

d. Check each of the following for proper operation, adjustments, or condition:

(1) Directional signals.

(2) Stop lights and signals.

(3) Special warning lights.

(4) Emergency flashers.

(5) Clearance and marker lights.

(6) Headlights.

(7) Interior bus lights.

(8) Stop arm control, if so equipped.

(9) Windshield fan and defroster.

(10) Heaters.

(11) Horn.

(12) Service door and control.

(13) Rear view and side view mirrors.

(14) Fuses and emergency equipment.

(15) Driver's seat.

(16) Driver's seat belt.

(17) Fire extinguisher.

(18) First aid kit.

(19) Wipers/washers.

(20) Sanders, when equipped.

2. Operating Inspection. A planned road check enables the driver to evaluate the steering, suspension, clutch, transmission, driveline, engine, and brakes. The following items should be included when "road checking" the vehicle prior to transporting pupils:

   a. The Parking Brake: check by slowly engaging the clutch while the parking brake is "on." (In some air brake systems, the parking brake will remain applied if there is a partial or complete air pressure loss in the service brakes.)

   b. Transmission Operation: an automatic transmission should not slip and a manual transmission should allow for easy and smooth gear changes throughout the entire shifting range.

   c. The Clutch: the clutch should engage easily and smoothly without jerking, slipping excessively, or "chattering." A properly adjusted clutch should have some "free play" when the pedal is fully released.

d. Service Brakes: test at low speeds—bring the bus to a complete stop. It should stop in a "straight line" . . . without skidding, swerving, or pulling to one side.

e. The Engine: never race a cold engine. Instead increase speed slowly so that all parts may be properly lubricated.

f. The Steering: report any unusual ride or handling characteristics.

g. The Suspension: report any unusual ride or handling characteristics.

Not all drivers have the ability to spot every problem. But all school bus drivers, however, should make a thorough stationary and operating inspection of their bus each day. "Inspection" to them becomes an integral part of driving and they are always alert to any warning signal which tells them something is wrong. This continued alertness permits them to spot trouble and act accordingly before that trouble causes serious damage or contributes to an accident.

E. Maintenance of Equipment.

1. Teamwork and written policies are essential to a well organized maintenance program.

   a. Strong and reasonable school bus maintenance policies should be adopted that will provide efficient guidelines for the following:

      (1) director of transportation.

      (2) maintenance personnel.

      (3) operators of the vehicles.

   b. Such policies should include the maintenance responsibilities of each person involved and should provide for a planned maintenance program.

2. Planned maintenance may be defined as scheduled maintenance that involves making minor repairs and adjustments which, if neglected, may develop into major difficulties, thereby necessitating extensive and expensive repairs in addition to the costly "down time."

   a. Manufacturers' service manuals and warranty protection guidelines contain valuable information for successful preventative maintenance programs. These instructions and procedures should be carefully followed for maximum efficiency and safety in fleet operation. Vehicle manufacturers and component suppliers (transmission, electrical, etc. manufacturers) offer excellent training for fleet mechanics. Those interested in efficient operations will take advantage of these outstanding training programs.

b. Objectives of a planned maintenance program:

(1) keeping the vehicles in safe and efficient operating condition.

(2) preventing road failures.

(3) conserving fuel.

(4) lowering the maintenance cost by reducing the need for major repairs or overhaul.

(5) extending the useful life of the vehicle and its components.

(6) enhancing the appearance of school buses.

3. School districts or private contractors should develop a system whereby written communication would allow interchange and feedback relative to maintenance work needed and maintenance work completed. An efficient system should include:

a. Drivers report form to initiate needed maintenance.

b. Mechanic certification of completed work.

c. Method of permanently recording repairs and maintenance history of each vehicle.

F. Records

1. Accident records. The following should be included on all school bus accident report forms:

a. A signed and dated statement from the driver concerning the particulars of the accident.

b. A description and estimate of damage costs to all vehicles.

c. A list of all persons injured, including home addresses and home phone numbers, a description of personal injuries, and appropriate narrative explanations.

d. A list of passengers and witnesses, including addresses and phone numbers. A signed statement by witnesses is desirable, if obtainable. (Cards for witness signatures and statement should be carried in bus at all times.)

e. A description of drivers involved including name, date of birth, sex, years of driving experience, license number, and occupation.

f. Cost of repairs and other type follow-up information should be added to the accident report wherever it is filed, i.e., in federal, state, or local offices, so that the record of the accident is complete. Other pertinent information relating to the accident that should be added later includes:

(1) disposition of any litigation.

(2) disposition of any summonses.

(3) net effects of all personal injuries sustained, including medical care, physician's fees, hospital expenses, etc.

(4) amount of property damage other than to vehicles involved

(5) action taken against the school bus driver, e.g., suspension or dismissal.

(6) summation of the driver's total accident record so that each completed report form will contain a listing of the total number of accidents that the driver has experienced.

2. Personnel Records. The following types of information should be maintained on all employees:

a. Employee

(1) application, including occupational history, present occupation, previous employment, age, sex, vehicle driving experience, marital status, military service record (if applicable), and formal training. (see Appendix B)

(2) confirmed work history.

(3) driving record.

(4) criminal record.

(5) military record (if applicable).

(6) physical examination (see Appendix C).

(7) training and testing.

(a) behind-the-wheel.

(b) knowledge.

(c) hours of instruction.

(8) payroll record.

(a) absences, cause.

(b) current wages.

(c) years of service.

(9) complaints, commendations, evaluations, etc.

b. Organizational

(1) number employed.

(2) number of staff employed by job.

(3) wage scales.

3. Route records

a. Type of routes.

(1) number.

(2) designation.

b. Route description.

(1) pickups, by locations and times.

(2) route time.

(3) type of vehicle required.

c. Route miles.

d. Special education pupils information to include medical history, medical procedures, and emergency phone numbers.

4. Maintenance records

a. Type.

(1) line setting tickets.

(2) work orders.

(3) preventative maintenance records.

b. Vehicle depreciation.

c. Equipment specifications.

5. Cost Records

a. vehicles.

b. type.

G. Emergency Procedures. Each school system should have an emergency plan. This plan should be carefully thought through and developed in cooperation with all those whose services would be required in the event of various types of emergencies. The school transportation director, school administrators, teachers, drivers, maintenance and service personnel, pupils, and others should be instructed in the procedures to be followed in the event of:

1. Accident. The plan should spell out precisely what is to be done, e.g., how to prevent further accidents; how to evacuate and control pupils; how to evaluate the need for medical assistance; how to get help from the police, the fire department, and the garage; and how to collect and record data essential to the preparation of the required accident reports. An operational plan to provide two-way communication with parents and/or guardians is imperative.

2. Sudden Disability of Driver. Procedures for handling situations resulting in the fatal injury or disability of the bus driver should be established and communicated to appropriate persons.

3. Road Failure. The emergency plan should cover the procedure for securing the bus, disposition and control of the passengers, diagnosing the cause(s) of the road failure, notification of school officials, securing alternate equipment, repair procedure and recovery of the disabled school bus.

4. Inclement Weather Conditions. The emergency plan should provide procedures for when the schools are to be closed or when the schools are to be closed early; the person responsible for making these decisions; how decisions are to be relayed to parents, pupil, school officials and staff (including teachers and cafeteria manager), drivers, contractors, maintenance and service personnel, the news media, and others. Other natural phenomena that might affect the school bus operation should also be included in the plan under this general heading, e.g., floods, hurricanes, and tornadoes.

5. Other Type of Emergency Situations. The emergency plan should cover such conditions and events as (a) civil defense drills; (b) strikes by school staff, teachers, drivers, or contractors; (c) road or bridge washouts and landslides that might block school bus routes; (d) bus hijacking. (Copies of the pre-emergency plan should be carried in each bus.) (See Appendix D for Instructions for Conducting Emergency Exit Drills.)

H. Communication. In the operation of a pupil transportation system, it is necessary to keep those who are in charge of the system as well as the parents and the pupils, informed regarding the operational procedures. The school system must ensure that the channels of communication are set up in such a way that any information that should be known about its transportation system and services can be disseminated quickly and effectively to reach everyone concerned. The school system must also ensure that all inquiries, requests, suggestions, and recommendations are given prompt and appropriate attention, and that they are handled efficiently. Some of the ways information regarding school bus systems can be disseminated satisfactorily, and examples of how each of these may be used to advantage are:

Method for Dissemination of Information	*Examples of Purposes for Which Used*
Bulletins:	To explain the school system's transportation policy to school administrators, teachers, drivers, parents, pupils, and others associated with the operation. To clarify new laws and safety policies so that everyone knows what is expected of them.
Meetings:	To provide an opportunity for those associated with the school transportation system to share their views to help build broad community support for safe pupil transportation.
Public Press:	To inform parents of policy, route, stop, and schedule changes; of the safety record of the operation; and positive driver achievement records.
Conferences:	To discuss with each driver, disruptive pupils and their parents, solutions to disciplinary problems that arise, new or revised policy decisions that affect drivers, contractors, pupils, and school administrators.
Letters:	To inform parents of all school and state regulations, new routes, etc. Reply to more urgent inquiries regarding pupil transportation safety, policy and procedures.
Telephone Calls:	To provide quick contact between bus drivers and the school, or between parents and the school in the event of urgent or emergency situations.
Radio, Television:	To inform the public of procedures the schools will follow in cases of severe weather conditions or other natural phenomena as well as new policies, laws, or controver-

	sial decisions regarding laws and specifications. Excellent for positive news, ideas, and achievement.
Public Address System:	Another tool the school personnel and drivers may utilize to communicate with pupils regarding all forms of safety reminders, rules, and school policy.

VIII. EVALUATION OF THE PUPIL TRANSPORTATION SYSTEM

A. Each school system should have a plan for evaluating its pupil transportation operation. (See Appendix H) There are several criteria which can be applied to obtain some estimates of the operation's effectiveness. These criteria relate to such factors as safety, efficiency, and economy.

1. Safety criteria include, but may not be limited to:

    a. Injuries to pupils, the driver, and other highway users.

    b. Frequency and severity of property damage accidents in which buses are involved.

    c. Frequency and severity of moving traffic violations for which drivers are cited.

    d. Frequency and nature of complaints from parents, the motoring public, school administrators and the pupils.

    e. Frequency and nature of road failures and other emergency situations involving buses.

2. Efficiency and economy criteria include, but may not be limited to:

    a. Route buses consistently operating within the framework of established school hours.

    b. Amount of driver layover time between routes. If, however, it can be scheduled, a brief layover period is desirable.

    c. Routes are equalized as nearly as possible and scheduled to minimize the actual time pupils are on the bus.

    d. Routes are designed to achieve maximum utilization, i.e., full capacity (within reason), and unnecessary mileage and duplication is eliminated.

    e. All routes and routing procedures including stops and times are reviewed annually.

    f. Written driver instructions, including pertinent information relative to mechanical operation and specifics, such as warm-up and idling times, braking practices, etc.

3. Problem identification criteria include, but may not be limited to comprehensive long and short range transportation plans, which include goals and a needs assessment. Information to assist school administration toward this end may be found in Appendix H, Needs Assessment Overview.

IX. ACTIVITY BUS OPERATIONS.

Each school system that provides activity bus transportation for pupils shall have comprehensive policies and guidelines regarding this type of transportation. In order to provide safe and efficient activity transportation, lines of responsibility and authority need to be defined. Persons involved in activity trips must have an understanding of their respective responsibilities. For the purpose of this section, activity trip is defined to include field trips which are extensions of the instructional program, and other trips such as athletic and other outings. This trips range from a few miles to trips extended over several days that cover large distances.

The following items need to be considered when developing criteria for activity trip transportation.

A. Policies and Guidelines

1. Purpose of trip—

   Instructional, athletic, pupil spectators' recreation, or other.

2. Funding source—

   District or individual school funds, individual charge, parent group or other.

3. Administrative approval—

   Person who has authority to approve or deny trip.

4. Advance notification—

   Allow adequate time for approval process, and for making driver and vehicle arrangements.

5. Methods of travel—

   District or contractor bus, commercial or local transit district equipment, air, boat, or combination of above, private or school passenger automobile.

6. Trip request form—

   This should include all necessary information from trip arrangements, payroll, reimbursement, and other local needs.

7. Chaperone—

   An adult chaperone should be required on all activity trips. Chaperone responsibilities include written authority to assist driver in maintaining passenger control. The drivers most always possess the final authority. Seating location for chaperones may also be a consideration.

8. Discipline procedures—

   Trip release signed by parents should include written procedures on handling of severe or difficult misbehavior problems, and emergency policies.

9. Communication—

   Drivers, pupils, chaperones and parents should be made aware of rules and regulations that apply on trip. Parents should have information on destination, mode of transportation, chaperones, departure and return times, and what the pupil is expected to wear and bring with them for the trip. A signed note from the parent or guardian is important.

10. Luggage—

    Method for transporting luggage or equipment forbidden to be carried in passenger compartment by state and/or local regulation. Loose luggage or equipment should never be transported in the passenger compartment which could cause injury or block passageways in the event of an accident or sudden maneuver.

11. Out-of-State Trips—

    Policy should detail if "out-of-state" trips are permitted and specific restrictions. Regulations for states to be visited should be reviewed prior to trip.

12. Insurance Policies—

    Should be checked or agents be contacted to determine if additional coverage is necessary. This is a necessity if a trip is scheduled to another state or country. If using transportation other than system owned vehicles, the board should set the minimum amount of insurance to be carried.

13. Road and Weather Check—

    Designate a person responsible for checking road conditions during months when adverse conditions could be encountered. State Patrol, Highway Divisions or auto clubs are generally cooperative in supplying road information. The Weather Bureau should also be contacted if warranted.

14. Contingency Plans—

    Policy should detail who has authority to make decisions if an unexpected occurrence happens during trip such as impassable roads, accident, or mechanical breakdown. Driver and chaperone should have phone number of local school person who has final authority. It is also advisable to obtain phone numbers of transportation personnel in various communities and school districts that trip buses travel through regularly. It is advisable to develop a Mutual Aid Directory for contacts within athletic league boundaries which could provide assistance in the event of a mechanical emergency. Drivers should have training on procedures and regulations if an accident occurs during trip.

15. Driving Hours—

    Schools should have regulations based on common sense and/or Bureau of Motor Carrier Safety manual: i.e., 15 hours of duty of which 10 are driving time; 8 hours continuous off-duty prior to long trip, no more than 60 hours driving in a week.

16. Driver Selection—

    Criteria for trip driver assignments is necessary to avoid conflict and confusion, knowledge, skill, experience, seniority and driver familiarity with trip vehicles. Driver knowledge of area to be traveled should also be a consideration. Driver assignment should take place at least 3 days in advance of trip date.

B. Vehicle and Equipment

1. Trip vehicles should be selected taking into consideration the following.

    a. Miles to be traveled.

    b. Terrain and climatic conditions which may be encountered.

    c. Number and age group of pupils.

    d. Luggage and equipment to be transported.

    e. Driver familiarity with the vehicle and route to be traveled.

2. Consideration should be given for specialized equipment needed such as:

    a. Luggage storage.

    b. Chains or sanders (chains should be prefitted prior to trip.)

c. Extra heaters.

d. Public address system.

e. Radio—A.M., C.B., or 2-way.

f. Tires, off road tread or recaps (original tires on front required).

g. Spare tire.

h. Tool requirements.

i. If an extended trip is planned, a phone call to transportation personnel at the destination is advisable to determine equipment requirements.

3. Inspection—

a. All vehicles should pass the same inspections as regular route buses as well as detailed check prior to activity trips.

C. Training

1. Specialized training should be provided for activity trip drivers. Training should include but may not be limited to the following items:

a. State laws and applicable policies and rules.

b. Familiarity with trip vehicle and its components.

c. Familiarity with specialized equipment and how to implement its use. (see B-2 above)

d. Familiarity with local and state trip requirements.

e. Route familiarization. This might include a dry run prior to the trip date, especially if extreme conditions, terrain or road difficulties may be encountered.

f. Discipline procedures on trips.

g. Driving under adverse conditions such as night driving, slippery road condition, or unfamiliar mountain driving.

h. Destination location and parking areas. Maps should be made available to drivers.

i. Destination parking if other than location of pupil destination.

j. Provisions for bus security at destination.

k. Necessity to carry extra cash for items such as: bridge tolls, fuel, telephone, parking fees, and personal needs.

l. Emergency procedures including a thorough knowledge of contingency requirements.

m. Other items a driver should know prior to driving an activity trip, e.g., pupil counts, report form completion, convoy procedures, prohibiting non-required signs inside or outside of bus, etc.

n. All activity bus drivers should hold the same licenses and certificates as a regular school bus driver. This might be in addition to a chauffeur's license if vehicle is a commercial carrier.

SPECIAL EDUCATION OPERATION

INTRODUCTION TO SPECIAL EDUCATION OPERATION

The purpose of this section of the report is to recommend minimum standard guidelines for those persons entrusted with the responsibility for transporting pupils requiring special care during the loading, unloading and transporting process. The term "special education" means specially designed courses of instruction and related support services, sufficient in both quantity and quality to meet the unique needs of handicapped children.

This section of the overall operations report is concerned with the identification of the multitude of practices and procedures that are relevant to the transportation of handicapped pupils. Special attention, for example, has been given to the development of general principles, the identification of the major characteristics of handicapped pupils, the noting of pupil needs relating to class placement, the behavioral actions that can be anticipated, the resulting corrective actions that must be taken, the types of medical concerns that must be dealt with in an efficient and professional manner, and the development of emergency pupil management procedures.

Few of the practices and procedures are discussed in detail. All, however, have been treated in sufficient depth to provide the administrator, the driver, and the aide with sufficient information to develop and administer a quality program service.

MINIMUM STANDARD GUIDELINES FOR SCHOOL BUS OPERATION: SPECIAL EDUCATION

INTRODUCTION

The term "special education" means specially designed instruction to meet the unique needs of a handicapped child. Transportation is one of the "related services" that is necessary to provide this instruction. The purpose of this document is to establish minimum standard guidelines of operation for those individuals involved in the transportation of the handicapped.

I. GENERAL PRINCIPLES

A. Pupil management encompasses all preparation and action taken to meet each pupil's needs while riding to and from school, in the interest of comfort and safety for all those aboard the bus. For the handicapped pupil, this means making a variety of adjustments to accommodate each one's individual needs without compromising the safety of the riders or the primary role of the driver—to drive the bus.

B. Transportation for handicapped pupils is a highly personalized service, requiring a thorough assessment of the pupils' physical, social, emotional, and intellectual capacities, and making allowances for existing handicaps.

C. Successful pupil management depends upon careful planning for each pupil's needs prior to placement and continued monitoring of the adjustments throughout the school year. Good pupil management techniques avoid the narrow, band aid approach of "What do I do when Johnny misbehaves on the bus?" by assessing needs and anticipating problems.

D. Mutual respect for, and communication and cooperation of drivers, parents, teachers, and other school officials will help to ensure safe, reliable, and comfortable transportation service. It is important to recognize that often the driver spends several hours a day with these pupils, thereby assuming a significant role in their lives.

II. CHARACTERISTICS OF HANDICAPPED PUPILS

A. The definition of the types of disabilities vary somewhat from State to State, but in general terms, the following behaviors are characteristic. Keep in mind that no one pupil is likely to manifest all of these behaviors.

1. Learning disabled pupils typically have average or higher intellectual ability, but suffer from disorders that prevent them from processing information, particularly language, in the usual manner. They may be disorganized or inefficient in solving problems. They may demonstrate impulsive or extreme emotional behaviors that seem out of proportion to the severity of the problem. Hyperactivity is also common among this population.

2. Emotionally disturbed pupils may have great difficulty controlling their own behavior. Emotional disturbance is characterized by very low self-esteem, and the pupil may either withdraw or act out his frustration and insecurity. Seemingly inappropriate types of duration of behavior may be observed, the seriousness of which should be discussed with the pupil's teacher. A limited number of clear, consistent rules will set goals for the pupil to regulate his own actions. Avoid angry outbursts and punishment, and never label a pupil "bad" when he/she misbehaves. Simply remind the pupil of what is expected and why, and reinforce proper behavior. A lack of stability from day to day in desirable behavior may be observed. This is not willful disobedience, but beyond the pupil's control.

3. Mental retardation encompasses a range of impairment from the mildly (educable) retarded through the trainable, and finally the severely and profoundly handicapped. Many pupils may have physical handicaps in addition to the mental handicaps, and may be afflicted by disorders involving poor motor coordination, seizures, and body tremors. Pupils may have few self-care skills,

and require aid in dressing, expressing themselves, and boarding the bus. They may be very friendly and affectionate. They need frequent reminders of bus rules because they have limited retention. Many pupils can understand what you tell them (possess receptive language) but cannot speak to you. You should insist that they use every mode of communication of which they are capable to make their needs known to you.

4. Physical handicaps can include deafness, blindness, paralysis, lack of head, trunk or back control, or erratic movement. These pupils may be of average or above intelligence, but are frequently behind in social and academic development due to their handicapping condition. Those with orthopedic handicaps often have leg braces, crutches, wheelchairs, or other supportive equipment. These pupils must be seated comfortably.

    a. Communication with pupils whose handicaps interfere with normal means of expression can pose a major challenge to the driver.

        (1) Visually handicapped pupils respond best when they are addressed by name, and when the events around them are described carefully. Remember that they cannot see facial expressions or other body language that constitutes a large part of communication for others. The visually impaired can develop self-sufficiency if their environment is structured in a stable and predictable way. They can fasten their own seat belts if they can find them on the same seat in the same position each day. They cannot easily recover them if they've fallen behind the seat, or if their seat changes and the seat belt is no longer there.

        (2) The deaf pupils use their visual skills to compensate for their hearing loss. Looking at them when you talk, and speaking clearly and distinctly will help them read your lips. Yelling does not help them understand. Facial expression and body language are very important; show them what you want. The drivers may wish to carry a pad and pencil to write down what the cannot otherwise convey. Those drivers who routinely transport deaf children may find a course in sign language valuable. Deaf children may find the noise level on their hearing aids uncomfortable, and turn them off. They will probably be most content if there are others on the bus with whom they can communicate. Hearing impaired children, along with visually impaired pupils, are unlikely to be much different from normal children in terms of behavioral problems.

B. Although the behaviors described above are characteristic of certain categories of disabling conditions, it is important to remember that each pupil is an individual, with his own distinct personality and that no label can completely or adequately describe any pupil. It should also be noted that all handicapped pupils are people, and can be expected to behave and misbehave very much like normal children. The driver of handicapped children needs to be more flexible, patient, and creative in his/her approach to managing these pupils.

III. CLASS PLACEMENT

A. Class selection should include a routine consultation with transportation personnel to avoid bus problems that may later develop into classroom problems.

1. Some pupils may need to be transported in wheelchairs or specially designed car seats or vests to provide trunk and head support. The type of vehicle required must be ascertained in advance, and lead time may be needed to construct a device in which to transport the pupil.

2. The last consideration in planning is the mixture of pupils on the vehicle. In sparsely populated areas, it may be virtually impossible to group pupils on vehicles by disability, but this may be desirable in some instances.

B. After the class assignment is determined, the transportation supervisor should research the details of the pupil's transportation needs.

1. A thorough inventory of the pupil's needs should be taken by the school personnel in conjunction with the transportation director. This should include aspects of the pupil's personality and handicaps as they relate to the bus ride, and may determine such matters as seat assignments, order of stops, equipment needed, and techniques for effectively relating to the pupil. Seizures and other significant medical problems should be documented.

2. At this time, any deviation from normal schedules should be noted.

3. Arrangements should be made for alternate emergency drop-off points and telephone numbers. These last two points may seem more related to operations than pupil management, but not delivering the pupil to the right place at the right time can create anxiety in the pupil and his parents and undermine the driver's control of the situation.

4. Arrangements for each pupil's transportation should be communicated to all involved parties, including parents, school personnel, driver, aide, and the other pupils on the bus. A smooth start for bus service will help make the pupil's first day of school a positive experience and will instill confidence in the parent that will reflect well on the entire school system.

IV. DISCIPLINE AND BEHAVIOR CONTROL

A. A driver recognizes that safety of passengers and respect for person and property are still needed when handicapped children are transported. A pupil cannot be allowed to behave in any manner which endangers others or causes serious harm enroute.

B. Lenience or pity for the pupils because of their handicaps is counterproductive to the development of self-sufficiency. Many pupils can sense this attitude and manipulate it to their own advantage. Pupils must be taught to accept responsibility for their own actions. This can usually be accomplished if the following rules are obeyed:

1. Always let the pupils know what is expected of them. Define terms and rules clearly, and enforce the rules fairly, firmly, and consistently.

2. Let the pupils know exactly what the consequences of their behavior will be. Always follow through on the disciplinary action you threaten, or the pupils will quickly learn that your authority is not to be taken seriously.

3. Demonstrate, using as many modes as possible, what you want them to do. Don't just tell them to fasten their restraining devices, show them how to do it.

4. Accentuate the positive. Continually telling the pupils "don't do this" and "don't do that" leaves them wondering what they can do. On long bus rides that can be a tiring and boring experience, suggest methods of acceptable behavior.

C. Behavior modification is a technique that requires pupils to behave in an appropriate way before they are given some reward, thereby increasing the likelihood they will behave as desired. To be effective, such a program must take into consideration the ages of the pupils aboard, the nature of the reward, and a clear definition of what constitutes acceptable behavior.

1. It is generally a good policy to develop a simple reward system for good behavior. Liberal amounts of praise should be given as a general rule, but behavior modification techniques can be a more concrete, consistent way of maintaining control.

2. The driver can develop a chart to keep track on a weekly basis of who has behaved well and who has not, and a reward given to those with satisfactory ratings. This may be something simple like a smile face or a gold star on the chart, giving the pupil a preferred seat on the bus, or, with permission of both parent and teacher, some candy or other treat.

3. Some disruptive pupils respond well when given responsibility, such as leading the others in singing or a quiet game. This may channel excess energy into some more constructive although

limited activity that can be pursued safely on the bus ride.

D. Other techniques of behavior control involve relatively simple methods such as rearranging seating or isolating the troublemaker.

1. Seating arrangements on the bus can be important in managing handicapped pupils. A good driver will learn to know his/her pupils and seat those who get along well near each other.

   a. The seat closest to the front of the vehicle may be used either as a reward or as a punishment, depending on the attitude of the pupils. Younger pupils often perceive sitting near the driver as a privilege, and this may be granted as a reward for good behavior. Older pupils are more likely to view a front seat as undesirable, and it may then be used to isolate a troublemaker.

   b. An insightful choice of seat partners can help the driver manage pupils. For instance, a young hyperactive pupil may be seated with an older, well-behaved pupil. The older pupil is made to feel important by looking after his young charge, and the younger pupil may look up to the elder and behave better to impress him. A more advanced pupil may be able to sit with one who is easily distractible to "entertain" the other by talking or looking at a book.

   c. Very young or fragile pupils should be seated away from older, larger pupils who might harm them if they become angry or frustrated.

2. In cases of serious misbehavior, temporary suspension of bus privileges may be in order. This should only be done after consultation with parent and teacher, because in some cases this may mean a pupil might be left home unsupervised, or an adolescent may spend the day out on the streets getting into trouble rather than being in school. Suspension from the bus is usually most appropriate when the safety of other pupils is threatened by the pupil in question.

3. Most pupils respond best to rules if they have a voice in developing them. The driver may be able to tell the pupils that the bus is "their bus" and to encourage pride in making it a clean, safe, and enjoyable place to be. For those pupils who are able, the driver may have them suggest rules for the bus and the means of enforcing them. Often the pupils will be more strict in determining regulations that the driver would have been.

4. Cases of serious misbehavior which do not respond to any of the above methods may require referral to a school counselor or psychologist to develop a more personalized behavior management scheme for that pupil.

5. Behavior management systems will be most effective if developed

after consultation with the parents and teachers. It can be confusing and frustrating to the pupils if they are allowed to behave one way on the bus but not that way in the classroom. Cooperation of all concerned parties is the ideal way to achieve a safe bus environment.

V. MEDICAL CONCERNS

A. Handicapped pupils are often more susceptible to illness than regular pupils, and therefore miss school more often. They are often on medication for their disability. Normally, a driver should never administer this medication. It is strongly recommended that drivers of handicapped pupils enroll in a first-aid course to prepare themselves for medical emergencies that may arise along the route.

B. A change in the type of dosage of medication can dramatically alter a pupil's behavior. Sudden personality changes should be reported to the parent and teacher at the earliest possible time.

C. There are certain medical problems that may arise routinely on the bus ride, for which a driver should be prepared.

1. Many handicapped children are subject to convulsive disorders, or seizures. These can vary in intensity from a few-second (petit mal) blackout, often not even noticeable, to severe grand mal seizures, involving thrashing of arms, and body rigidity. Normally, seizures are self-limiting, and the driver's primary role should be to see that the pupil does not harm him/herself and rests comfortably afterward. Nothing should be placed in the pupil's mouth, nor should the limbs be restrained in any manner—this could result in broken bones. Extended seizures constitute a medical emergency, and medical help should be summoned.

2. Some pupils may be inclined toward respiratory difficulties and drooling, and may occasionally choke on their own saliva or foreign objects. The method of dealing with these problems should be discussed with the parent, teacher and medical personnel. Pupils may become nauseated on the bus ride so it is recommended that materials for clean-up be kept on the vehicle.

D. Most medical incidents on the bus ride, while requiring special attention of the driver or aide, will not necessitate summoning professional medical attention. Extended seizures and other serious medical matters may require either diverting the run to a medical facility or summoning an ambulance. In any event, all medically related incidents should be reported to the school and parents at the earliest possible moment.

VI. EMERGENCY PUPIL MANAGEMENT

A. It may be useful to educate those pupils who are capable of comprehending and retaining such information about emergency procedures.

It is possible that the driver may be incapacitated in an accident and a pupil may have to take over.

B. In those emergencies where the driver is not injured, it is important to assure the pupils that the situation is under control.

C. The most important preparation for pupil management in an emergency is preplanning.

1. Assess the abilities and handicaps of each pupil, and determine what each pupil's needs may be in an emergency.

2. Plan how to evacuate each pupil if this becomes necessary, determine what special attention might be needed after evacuation. For instance, those pupils normally tense and insecure may require special reassurance than what would be required for most pupils under such circumstances. The appearance of confidence on the part of the driver will help calm the pupils.

VII. SUMMARY OF SUCCESSFUL PUPIL MANAGEMENT

A. Take a conscious inventory of the abilities and handicapping conditions of each pupil, and gear the rules of the bus to each individual bus load of pupils.

B. Continuity and consistency of expectations by those in authority at home, in the classroom, and on the bus, will do much to aid the pupil in his social development, independence, self-esteem, and recognition and respect for the rights of others.

POLICY DEVELOPMENT

Develop pupil, driver and aide policies.

PUPIL POLICY:

1. Develop a written list of do's and don't's that you expect pupils to be aware of to ensure a safer, more enjoyable ride.

    A. Post in the bus.

    B. Print in pupil handbook.

    C. This may be written into an overall policy package that should have board approval.

DRIVER POLICY:

1. List all requirements that must be fulfilled prior to pupil transportation (license, physical, driving exam, written exams, license check, etc.).

2. List all requirements placed on the driver by the school system. Examples:

    A. Pre-trip inspection.

    B. Discipline.

    C. Records keeping.

    D. Contract provision, if any.

    E. Pupil safety.

    F. Knowledge and use of safety equipment.

3. List all requirements placed on the driver by state and/or federal legislation. Examples:

    A. School bus stop laws.

    B. Speed limits.

    C. Railroad crossing laws.

    D. Etc.

An entire policy package should be developed, approved and adopted by the Board of Education and implemented.

AIDE POLICY:

Aides should:

1. Be selected for their physical and emotional ability to cope with the situation(s) making the assignment of an aide to that particular bus necessary.

2. Receive special training regarding the needs of handicapped pupils and their role in caring for those needs in transit.

3. Work under the bus driver's direction to provide care and assistance to pupils as needed when entering and leaving the bus and during the bus ride.

4. Be sure that protective safety devices are properly fastened at all times.

5. Have available to them in the vehicle confidential data including:

   A. Pupil's name and address.

   B. Nature of pupil's handicap.

   C. Emergency health care information.

   D. Name and the phone number of pupil's physician, parent, or other person to be contacted in case of an emergency.

   E. Provisions for pupil's welfare if and when pupil is not met at the designated bus stop.

6. Be well versed in emergency procedures in the event the driver is incapacitated.

ROUTING AND SCHEDULING

1. Determine location and destination of all pupils to be transported.

2. Obtain information pertaining to individual needs for additional specialized equipment such as safety harnesses, seat belts, wheelchair, pupil safety seat, etc.

3. Plot the safest, most efficient route available avoiding high traffic areas, high accident areas, and road hazards.

4. Provide the drivers, the attending school, and the transportation office with the following information:

   A. List of pupils on the bus(es).

   B. Approximate times for pick-up and return of pupils.

C. Map indicating routing of the bus and location of pupils.

D. An identification form for each pupil with information such as pupil's name, parent or guardian name, address, phone number, location and description of home, medication, picture, etc.

5. Provide the parents or guardians of all pupils with the driver's name, bus number, pick-up and return times, school closing information, school calendar, etc.

6. Transportation of pupils in certain cases may require a contract between school systems and/or specifications of transportation in the pupil's I.E.P. (Individual Education Plan).

7. If computer scheduling is available, it should be assessed for possible utilization.

8. The goal of pupil transportation is to economically and efficiently operate with the optimum pupil safety and consistency.

COMMUNICATION

1. Determine what your schools needs are for communications.

2. Determine the geographical area to be covered and topographical features to contend with.

3. Determine which type of two way radio system, if used, will be functional.

SCHOOL BUS STANDARDS

CONTENTS

2

SCHOOL BUS STANDARDS

OBJECTIVES AND GUIDING PRINCIPLES

Since the first National Conference on school bus standards in 1939, certain objectives and guiding principles have had a vital role in the development of the minimum standards for school buses. These objectives and guiding principles have been reaffirmed and emphasized at the subsequent National Conferences. The two major objectives, safety and economy, along with the following principles, have served as guide-posts for making decisions on the minimum standards and in arriving at sound and common agreement.

OBJECTIVES

The transportation of pupils in safety and comfort on safe, economical vehicles can be assured through adequate state regulations governing school bus construction.

Safety includes all those factors relating to the school bus construction which may directly or indirectly affect the safety and welfare of pupils transported.

Economy includes the construction, procurement, operation, and maintenance of school buses consistent with the safety and welfare of the pupils.

GUIDING PRINCIPLES

1. Uniform state school bus standards should:

    a. Be consistent with the objectives of safety and economy.

    b. Eliminate the construction of unsafe buses.

    c. Reduce conflicting standards wherever possible among states in the interest of production efficiency.

d. Specify exact dimensions where necessary to increase the efficiency of volume production.

e. Eliminate unnecessary luxury consistent with the safety and welfare of pupils transported.

2. Any adaptation of the nationally recommended minimum standards should be made by states only in order to permit desirable adjustments to local needs and only when such adaptations do not:

   a. Basically conflict with the recommended National Minimum Standards.

   b. Otherwise unduly increase production costs.

3. Uniform state standards for school buses should specify results desired in terms of safety and economy, and these performance specifications must be defined when this is necessary to make the regulations enforceable.

4. Provisions should be made for periodic review and revision of uniform state standards for school buses through cooperation of the states.

5. Uniform state standards for school buses should permit opportunities for the use of new inventions and improvements which are consistent with safety and economy.

6. Uniform state standards for school bus construction should provide for a degree of flexibility within which sound construction is possible (consistent with safety and economy) to accomodate the various manufacturers.

7. Uniform state standards for school bus construction should recognize that the actual designing of school buses is a responsibility of the manufacturers.

8. The current National Minimum Standards for School Buses are considered in full force and effect as recommendations to the states. Revisions of these standards are made only when evidence indicates that such revisions are needed.

USING THESE MINIMUM STANDARDS

In order that these minimum standards for school buses may be put into effect, each state legislature which has not already done so should confer upon the appropriate state agency the general responsibility for setting up statewide rules and regulations regarding the construction of school bus chassis, bodies and equipment. Detailed standards for school buses or their operations should not be written into state law.

The minimum standards for school buses appearing in this report must be officially adopted by the appropriate state agency to become legally effective within that state.

These minimum standards are intended to apply primarily to new vehicles, including all types of school buses as defined in the section entitled, Definitions, School Bus (Type A, Type B, Type C, Type D). It should be noted here that vehicles with a capacity for less than 10 passengers cannot be certified as school buses under federal regulations.

These minimum standards are not intended to apply to buses used primarily as public carriers rather than to transport pupils to and from school.

States should normally allow at least six (6) months lead time between publication of specifications and effective date. The effective date should be expressed:

> "These specifications apply respectively to chassis and bodies placed in production after (month, date, year)."

INTRODUCTION TO SCHOOL BUS STANDARDS

This portion of the book is divided into two sections: Chassis Standards and Body Standards. There are two basic reasons for this format: (1) to define minimum chassis and body standards, and (2) to assign responsibility for providing the defined equipment. Items in the chassis standards are to be provided by the chassis manufacturer; items in the body standards are to be provided by the body manufacturers.

Every attempt has been made by the Writing Committees, the Conference itself, and the Editing Committees to eliminate conflicts between these specifications and federal regulations. Should conflicts be found or arise through new federal regulations or legally binding interpretations of those regulations they should be brought to the attention of the Interim Committee.

For new vehicles, it is the responsibility of the vehicle manufacturers to certify compliance with applicable federal standards by installing a certification plate in the driver's area on each vehicle. However, as the vehicle is maintained over its useful life, it is the responsibility of those who supervise and perform work on the vehicle to assure on-going compliance with all applicable standards. For this reason, maintenance personnel training, quality components, quality workmanship and thorough maintenance records are absolutely essential.

As the title of this document suggests, these are intended to be minimum standards. However, it is in the interest of the entire school bus industry to maintain uniformity in certain basic areas such as vehicle identification. This concept was endorsed by the conference by deciding to tighten color tolerances on National School Bus Glossy Yellow and by deciding to standardize on an eight light warning system.

Finally, in order to insure that specifications are being met by manufacturers, states are urged to adopt and carry out effective pre-delivery inspection programs. This will promote safety as well as uniformity of compliance with specifications.

DEFINITIONS, SCHOOL BUS

TYPE A—

A Type "A" school bus is a conversion or body constructed upon a van-type compact truck or a front-section vehicle, with a gross weight rating of 10,000 pounds or less, designed for carrying more than 10 persons.

TYPE B—

A Type "B" school bus is a conversion or body constructed and installed upon a van or front-section vehicle chassis, or stripped chassis, with a vehicle weight rating of more than 10,000 pounds, designed for carrying more than 10 persons. Most of the engine is beneath and/or behind the windshield and beside the driver's seat. The entrance door is behind the front wheels.

TYPE C—

A Type "C" school bus is a body installed upon a flat back cowl chassis with a gross vehicle weight rating of more than 10,000 pounds, designed for carrying more than 10 persons. All of the engine is in front of the windshield and the entrance door is behind the front wheels.

TYPE D—

A Type "D" school bus is a body installed upon a chassis, with the engine mounted in the front, midship, or rear, with a gross vehicle weight rating of more than 10,000 pounds, designed for carrying more than 10 persons. The engine may be behind the windshield and beside the driver's seat; it may be at the rear of the bus, behind the rear wheels, or midship between the front and rear axles. The entrance door is ahead of the front wheels.

6

CHASSIS STANDARDS
THE BUS CHASSIS

AIR CLEANER

1. The engine intake air cleaner shall be furnished and properly installed by the chassis manufacturer to meet engine specifications.

AXLES

1. The front and rear ends including suspension assemblies shall have a gross axle weight rating at ground at least equal to that portion of the load as would be imposed by the chassis manufacturer's maximum gross vehicle weight rating.

BRAKES

1. A braking system, including service brake and parking brake, shall be provided.

2. Buses using air or vacuum in the operation of the brake system shall be equipped with warning signals, readily audible and visible to the driver, that will give a continuous warning when the air pressure available in the system for braking is 60 psi (pounds per square inch) or less or the vacuum in the system available for braking is eight inches (8) of mercury or less. An illuminated gauge that will indicate to the driver the air pressure in pounds per square inch or the inches of mercury vacuum available for the operation of the brakes shall be provided.

    a. Vacuum-assist brake systems shall have a reservoir used exclusively for brakes that shall be adequate to ensure loss in vacuum at full stroke application of not more than 30 per cent with the engine not running. Brake system on gas-powered engines shall include suitable and convenient connections for the installation of a separate vacuum reservoir.

    b. Any brake system dry reservoir shall be so safeguarded by a check valve or equivalent device, that in the event of failure or leakage in its connection to the source of compressed air or vacuum, the stored dry air or vacuum shall not be depleted by the leakage or failure.

3. Buses using a hydraulic assist-booster in the operation of the brake system shall be equipped with warning signals, readily audible and visible to the driver, that will provide continuous warning in the event of a loss of fluid flow from primary source.

4. The brake lines and booster-assist lines shall be protected from excessive heat and vibration and be so installed as to prevent chafing.

5. All brake systems shall be designed to permit visual inspection of brake lining wear without removal of any chassis components.

BUMPER, FRONT

1. Front bumper shall be furnished by chassis manufacturer as part of the chassis.

2. Front bumper shall extend beyond forward-most part of body, grille, hood, and fenders and shall extend to outer edges of fenders at bumper top line.

3. Front bumper, except breakaway bumper ends shall be of sufficient strength to permit pushing a vehicle of equal gross vehicle weight without permanent distortion to bumper, chassis, or body.

EXCEPTION: Type "D" Vehicle (Transit) front bumper shall be furnished by body manufacturer.

CERTIFICATION

1. Chassis manufacturer will, upon request, certify to the state agency having pupil transportation jurisdiction that their product meets minimum standards on items not covered by certification issued under requirements of the National Traffic and Motor Vehicle Safety Act.

CLUTCH

1. Clutch torque capacity shall be equal to or greater than the engine torque output.

COLOR

1. Chassis, including wheels and front bumper, shall be black; hood, cowl, and fenders shall be in National School Bus yellow. (See Appendix)

EXCEPTION: Hood may be painted low-luster yellow.

DRIVE SHAFT

1. Drive shaft shall be protected by a metal guard or guards around circumference of the drive shaft to reduce the possibility of it whipping through the floor or dropping to the ground if broken.

ELECTRICAL SYSTEM

1. <u>Battery</u>

    a. Storage battery shall have a minimum cold cranking capacity rating equal to the cranking current required for 30 seconds at 0° Farenheit (−17.8c) and a minimum reserve capacity rating of 120 minutes at 25 amp. Higher capacities may be required dependent upon optional equipment and local environmental conditions.

b. When a battery is to be mounted by the body manufacturer on a sliding tray as opposed to the standard installation provided by the chassis manufacturer, the battery shall be temporarily mounted on the chassis frame by the chassis manufacturer. In this case the final location of the battery and the appropriate cable lengths shall be according to the SBMI Design Objectives Booklet, 1980 edition (see Appendix).

2. Generator or Alternator

a. Type A bus shall have a minimum 60 ampere per hour alternator.

b. Type B bus shall have a minimum 80 ampere per hour alternator.

c. Type C and D buses shall have a generator or alternator with a minimum rating of at least 80 amperes (in accordance with Society of Automotive Engineers rating—see appendix) with minimum charging of 30 amperes at manufacturer's recommended engine idle speed (12 volt system), and shall be ventilated and voltage-controlled and, if necessary, current-controlled.

d. Type A, B, C, and D buses, equipped with an electrical power lift, shall have a minimum 100 ampere per hour alternator.

e. Direct-drive generator or alternator is permissible in lieu of belt drive. Belt drive shall be capable of handling the rated capacity of the generator or alternator with no detrimental effect on other driven components.

f. Refer to SBMI Design Objectives, May 1980 edition (see Appendix), for estimating required generator or alternator capacity.

3. Wiring

a. General—All wiring shall conform to current applicable recommended practices of the Society of Automotive Engineers (see appendix).

(1) All wiring shall use a standard color coding and each chassis shall be delivered with a wiring diagram that coincides with the wiring of the chassis.

b. Chassis manufacturer shall install a readily accessible terminal strip or plug on the body side of the cowl, or at accessible location in engine compartment of vehicles designed without a cowl, that shall contain the following terminals for the body connections:

(1) Main 100 amp body circuit.

(2) Tail lamps.

(3) Right turn signal.

(4) Left turn signal.

(5) Stop lamps.

(6) Back up lamps.

(7) Instrument panel lights (rheostat controlled by headlamp switch).

EXHAUST SYSTEM

1. Exhaust pipe, muffler, and tailpipe shall be outside bus body compartment and attached to chassis.

2. Tailpipe shall be constructed of a corrosion-resistant tubing material at least equal in strength and durability to 16 gauge steel tubing.

3. Tailpipe shall (a) extend beyond rear axle and shall extend at least 5 inches beyond chassis frame and be mounted outside of chassis frame rail at end point or (b) may extend to, but not beyond the body limits on the left side of the bus, behind the driver's compartment, outboard of chassis center line and shall terminate from chassis centerline as follows:

Type A vehicles	—Manufacturer's standard
Type B vehicles	—42.5 inches
Type C and D vehicles	—48.5 inches

EXCEPTION: The exhaust system on vehicles designed for the transportation of special education pupils shall be routed to the left of the right frame rail to allow for the installation of a lift on the right side of the vehicle.

4. Exhaust system on gas-powered chassis shall be properly insulated from fuel tank connections by a securely attached metal shield at any point where it is 12 inches or less from tank or tank connections.

5. Muffler shall be constructed of corrosion-resistant material.

FENDERS, FRONT, TYPE C VEHICLES

1. Total spread of outer edges of front fenders, measured at fender line, shall exceed total spread of front tires when front wheels are in straight-ahead position.

2. Front fenders shall be properly braced and free from any body attachments.

   EXCEPTION: Standard not applicable to Type A, B, and D vehicles.

FRAME

1. Frame or equivalent shall be of such design and strength characteristics as to correspond at least to standard practice for trucks of same general load characteristics which are used for highway service.

2. Any secondary manufacturer that modifies the original chassis frame shall guarantee the performance of workmanship and materials resulting from such modification.

3. Any frame modification shall not be for the purpose of extending the wheelbase.

4. Holes in top or bottom flanges of frame side rail shall not be permitted except as provided in original chassis frame. There shall be no welding to frame side rails except by chassis or body manufacturer.

5. Frame lengths shall be provided in accordance with SMBI Design Objectives, May 1980 edition. (See Appendix)

FUEL TANK

1. Fuel tank or tanks of minimum 30 gallon capacity with a 25 gallon actual draw shall be provided by the chassis manufacturer. It/they shall be filled and vented to the outside of the body, the location of which shall be so that accidental fuel spillage will not drip or drain on any part of the exhaust system.

2. No portion of the fuel system which is located to the rear of the engine compartment, except the filler tube, shall extend above the top of the chassis frame rail. Fuel lines shall be mounted to obtain maximum possible protection from the chassis frame.

3. Fuel filter with replaceable element shall be installed between fuel tank and engine.

4. Fuel tank installation shall be in accordance with SBMI Design Objectives, May 1980 edition. (See Appendix)

5. If a tank size other than 30 gallon is supplied, location of front of tank and filler spout must remain as specified by SBMI Design Objectives, May 1980 edition. (See Appendix)

   EXCEPTION: On vehicles constructed for transporting handicapped pupils, the fuel tank may be mounted on left chassis frame rail or behind rear wheels.

GOVERNOR

1. An engine governor is permissible. However, when it is desired to limit road speed, road-speed governor should be installed.

2. When engine is remotely located from driver, governor shall be installed to limit engine speed to maximum revolutions per minute recommended by engine manufacturer, or tachometer shall be installed so engine speed may be known to driver.

HEATING SYSTEM, PROVISION FOR

1. The chassis engine shall have plugged openings for the purpose of supplying hot water for the bus heating system. The opening shall be suitable for attaching ¾ inch pipe thread/hose connector. The engine shall be capable of supplying water having a temperature of at least 170°F at a flow rate of 50 pounds/per minute at the return end of 30 feet of one inch inside diameter automotive hot water heater hose. (SBMI Standard No. 001—Standard Code for Testing and Rating Automotive Bus Hot Water Heating and Ventilating Equipment.)

HORN

1. Bus shall be equipped with horn or horns of standard make, each horn capable of producing complex sound in bands of audio frequencies between 250 and 2,000 cycles per second and tested per Society of Automotive Engineers Standard J-377. (See Appendix)

INSTRUMENTS AND INSTRUMENT PANEL

1. Chassis shall be equipped with the following instruments and gauges. (Lights in lieu of gauges are not acceptable except as noted):

    a. Speedometer.

    b. Odometer which will give accrued mileage including tenths of miles.

    c. Voltmeter.

        (1) Ammeter with graduated charge and discharge with ammeter and its wiring compatible with generating capacities is permitted in lieu of voltmeter.

    d. Oil-pressure gauge.

    e. Water temperature gauge.

    f. Fuel gauge.

    g. Upper beam headlight indicator.

h. Brake indicator gauge. (vacuum or air).

(1) Light indicator in lieu of gauge permitted on vehicle equipped with hydraulic-over-hydraulic brake system.

i. Turn signal indicator.

2. All instruments shall be easily accessible for maintenance and repair.

3. Above instruments and gauges shall be mounted on instrument panel in such a manner that each is clearly visible to driver while in normal seated position in accordance with SBMI Design Objectives, May 1980 edition. (See Appendix)

4. Instrument panel shall have lamps of sufficient candlepower to illuminate all instruments and gauges and shift selector indicator for automatic transmission.

OIL FILTER

1. Oil filter of replaceable element or cartridge type shall be provided and shall be connected by flexible oil lines if it is not of built-in or engine mounted design. Oil filter shall have capacity of approximately one (1) quart.

OPENINGS

1. All openings in floorboard or firewall between chassis and passenger-carrying compartment, such as for gearshift lever and parking brake lever, shall be sealed.

PASSENGER LOAD

1. Actual gross vehicle weight (GVW) is the sum of the chassis weight, plus the body weight, plus the driver's weight, plus total seated pupil weight.

a. For purposes of calculation, the driver's weight is 150 pounds.

b. For purposes of calculation, the pupil weight is 120 pounds per pupil.

2. Actual Gross Vehicle Weight (GVW) shall not exceed the chassis manufacturer's gross vehicle weight rating (GVWR) for the chassis.

3. Manufacturer's gross vehicle weight rating shall be furnished in duplicate (unless more are requested) by manufacturer to the state agency having pupil transportation jurisdiction. State agency shall, in turn, transmit such ratings to each other state agency responsible for development or enforcement of state standards for school buses.

POWER AND GRADEABILITY

1. Gross Vehicle Weight (GVW) shall not exceed 185 pounds per net published horsepower of the engine at the manufacturer's recommended maximum number of revolutions per minute.

SHOCK ABSORBERS

1. Bus shall be equipped with front and rear double-acting shock absorbers compatible with manufacturer's rated axle capacity at each wheel location.

SPRINGS

1. Capacity of springs or suspension assemblies shall be commensurate with chassis manufacturer's gross vehicle weight rating.

2. If rear springs are used, they shall be of progressive type.

STEERING GEAR

1. Steering gear shall be approved by chassis manufacturer and designed to assure safe and accurate performance when vehicle is operated with maximum load and at maximum speed.

2. Steering mechanism shall provide for easy adjustment for lost motion.

3. No changes shall be made in steering apparatus which are not approved by chassis manufacturer.

4. There shall be clearance of at least 2 inches between steering wheel and cowl instrument panel, windshield, or any other surface.

5. Power steering is optional.

6. The steering system shall be designed to provide for means for lubrication of all wear-points.

TIRES AND RIMS

1. Tires and rims of proper size and tires with load rating commensurate with chassis manufacturer's gross vehicle weight rating shall be provided.

2. Dual rear tires shall be provided on Type B, Type C, and Type D school buses.

3. All tires on any given vehicle shall be of same size and ply rating.

4. If vehicle is equipped with spare tire and rim assembly, it shall be of the same size as those mounted on the vehicle.

5. If tire carrier is required, it shall be suitably mounted in accessible location outside passenger compartment.

TRANSMISSION

1. When automatic or semi-automatic transmission is used, it shall provide for not less than three forward speeds and one reverse speed.

2. When manual transmission is used, second gear and higher shall be synchronized except when incompatible with engine power. A minimum of three forward speeds and one reverse speed must be provided.

TURNING RADIUS

1. Chassis with a wheel base of 264 inches or less shall have a right and left turning radius of not more than 42½ feet, curb to curb measurement.

2. Chassis with a wheelbase of 265 inches or more shall have a right and left turning radius of not more than 44½ feet, curb to curb measurement.

UNDERCOATING

1. Chassis manufacturer shall coat undersides of front fenders (unless fenders are constructed of a non-corrosion material) with compound to prevent rust which meets or exceeds Federal Specifications TT–C–520a (see Appendix), using modified test procedures as defined under "Undercoating" of body standards.

WEIGHT DISTRIBUTION

1. Weight distribution of fully loaded bus on level surface shall be such so as not to exceed the manufacturer's front Gross Axle Weight Rating and rear Gross Axle Weight Rating.

BODY STANDARDS

THE BUS BODY

AISLE

1. Minimum clearance of all aisles shall be 12 inches. EXCEPTION: Type A Vehicle

2. The seat backs shall be slanted sufficiently to give aisle clearance of 15 inches at tops of seat backs.

BATTERY

1. Battery is to be furnished by chassis manufacturer.

2. When battery is mounted as described in Electrical System 1, Battery of Chassis Standard, the body manufacturer shall securely attach battery on slide-out or swing-out tray in a closed, vented compartment in the body skirt, whereby battery may be exposed to outside for convenient servicing. Battery compartment door or cover shall be hinged at front or top and secured by adequate and conveniently operated latch or other type fastener.

BUMPER (FRONT)

See Chassis Section

BUMPER (REAR)

1. Bumper shall be of pressed steel channel or equivalent material at least $\frac{3}{16}$-inch thick and 8 inches wide (high), and of sufficient strength to permit pushing by another vehicle without permanent distortion.

2. It shall be wrapped around back corners of bus. It shall extend forward at least 12 inches, measured from rear-most point of body at floor line.

3. Bumper shall be attached to chassis frame in such manner that it may be easily removed, shall be so braced as to develop full strength of bumper section from rear or side impact, and shall be so attached as to prevent hitching of rides.

4. Bumper shall extend at least one inch beyond rear-most part of body surface measured at floor line. EXCEPTION: Type A Vehicles

CEILING

See Insulation and Interior

CHAINS

See Wheelhousing

COLOR

The school bus body shall be painted a uniform National School Bus Yellow. (See Appendix)

The body exterior paint trim, bumper, lamp hoods (if any) emergency door arrow, and lettering shall be black. As an alternative, the rear bumper may be covered with reflective material.

CONSTRUCTION

1. Construction shall be of prime commercial quality steel or other metal or material with strength at least equivalent to all-steel as certified by bus body manufacturer.

2. Construction shall provide reasonably dustproof and water-tight unit.

DEFROSTERS

1. Defrosting and defogging equipment shall direct a sufficient flow of heated air onto the windshield, the window to the left of the driver and the glass in the viewing area directly to the right of the driver to reduce the amount of frost, fog and snow. The defroster unit shall have a separate blower motor in addition to the heater motors. EXCEPTION: Type A Vehicles

2. The defrosting system shall conform to Society of Automotive Engineers Standards J-381 and 382. (See Appendix)

3. The defroster and defogging system shall be capable of furnishing heated outside ambient air except that part of the system furnishing additional air to the windshield, entrance door and step-well may be of the recirculating air type.

4. Auxiliary fans are not to be considered as a defrosting and defogging system.

5. Portable heaters may not be used.

6. Auxiliary Fans—If Used

    a. Auxiliary fan for the left side shall be placed in a location where it can be adjusted to its maximum effectiveness.

    b. Auxiliary fan for the right side shall be in a location where it can be adjusted to its maximum effectiveness.

    c. These fans shall be a nominal six-inch diameter.

    d. The blades of these fans shall be covered with a protective cage. Each of these fans shall be controlled by a separate switch.

DOORS

1. Service Door:

   a. Service door shall be under control of driver, and designed so as to afford easy release and prevent accidental opening. When hand lever is used, no part shall come together so as to shear or crush fingers.

   b. Service door shall be located on right side of bus opposite driver and within direct view of driver.

   c. Service door shall have minimum horizontal opening of 24 inches and minimum vertical opening of 68 inches. EXCEPTION: Type A Vehicles

   d. Service door shall be of split type, sedan type, or jack-knife type. (Split-type door includes any sectioned door which divides and opens inward or outward.) If one section of split-type door opens inward and the other opens outward, front section shall open outward.

   e. Lower as well as upper panels shall be of approved safety glass. Bottom of lower glass panel shall not be more than 35 inches from ground when bus is unloaded. Top of upper glass panel shall not be more than 6 inches from top of door. EXCEPTION: Type A Vehicles

   f. Vertical closing edges shall be equipped with flexible material to protect children's fingers. EXCEPTION: Type A Vehicles

   g. There shall be no door to left of driver. EXCEPTION: Type A Vehicles

   h. All doors shall be equipped with a padding at the top edge of each door opening. Pad shall be at least 3 inches wide and 1 inch thick and extend the full width of the door opening.

2. Emergency Doors:

   a. Emergency door shall be hinged on right side if in rear end of bus and on front side if on left side of bus. It shall open outward and shall be labeled inside to indicate how it is to be opened. EXCEPTION: Type A and B Vehicles

   b. Upper portion of emergency door shall be equipped with approved safety glazing, exposed area of which shall be not less than 400 square inches.

   c. There shall be no steps leading to emergency door.

d. Words "EMERGENCY DOOR", both inside and outside in letters at least 2 inches high, shall be placed at top of or directly above the emergency door or on the door in the metal panel above the top glass.

FIRE EXTINGUISHERS

1. The bus shall be equipped with at least one pressurized, dry chemical-type fire extinguisher, mounted in a bracket and located in the driver's compartment and readily accessible to the driver. A pressure guage shall be mounted on the extinguisher as to be easily read without removing the extinguisher from its mounted position.

2. The fire extinguisher shall be of a type approved by the Underwriters Laboratories, Inc. (See Appendix) with a total rating of not less than 2 A-10 BC. The operating mechanism shall be sealed with a type of seal which will not interfere with the use of the fire extinguisher.

FIRST AID KIT

1. Bus shall have a removable, moisture and dustproof first-aid kit mounted in an accessible place within driver's compartment. This place shall be marked to indicate its location.

2. Number of units and contents shall be designated by proper state authorities from, but not limited to, the following items:
   2 single units—1-inch × 2½ yards adhesive tape
   2 single units—sterile gauze pads 3 in. × 3 in. (12 per unit)
   1 single unit—¾ in. × 3 in. adhesive bandage (100 per unit)
   1 single unit—2″ bandage compress (12 per unit)
   1 single unit—3″ bandage compress (12 per unit)
   2 single units—2″ × 6 yds. sterile gauze roller bandage
   2 single units—nonsterile triangular bandage approximately 40 in. × 36 in. × 54 in. with 2 safety pins
   3 single units—sterile gauze 36 in. × 36 in. (U.S.P. 2428 count)
   3 single units—sterile eye pad (1 per unit) 1 pair scissors

FLOOR

Floor in underseat area, including tops of wheelhousing, driver's compartment, and toeboard, shall be covered with rubber floor covering or equivalent having minimum overall thickness of .125 inch.

Floor covering in aisle shall be of aisle-type rubber or equivalent, wear-resistant, and ribbed. Minimum overall thickness shall be .187 inch measured from tops of ribs.

Floor covering must be permanently bonded to floor and must not crack when subjected to sudden changes in temperature. Bonding or adhesive material shall be waterproof and shall be of type recommended by manufacturer of floor-covering material. All seams must be sealed with waterproof sealer.

HEATERS

1. Heaters shall be of hot-water type or combustion type.

2. If only one heater is used, it shall be of fresh-air or combination fresh-air and recirculating type.

3. If more than one heater is used, additional heaters may be of recirculating air type.

4. The heating system shall be capable of maintaining throughout the bus temperature of not less than 40 degrees fahrenheit at average minimum January temperature as established by the U.S. Department of Commerce, Weather Bureau, for the area in which the vehicle is to be operated.

5. All heaters installed by body manufacturers shall bear a name plate that shall indicate the heater rating in accordance with SBMI Code 001, with said plate to be affixed by the heater manufacturer which shall constitute certification that the heater performance is as shown on the plate. EXCEPTION: Does not apply to vehicles not originally manufactured as school buses.

6. Heater hoses shall be adequately supported to guard against excessive wear due to vibration. The hoses shall not dangle or rub against the chassis or sharp edges and shall not interfere with or restrict the operation of any engine function. Heater hose shall conform to SAE J20c. Heater lines on the interior of bus shall be shielded to prevent scalding of the driver or passengers.

7. Each hot water heater system shall include a shutoff valve installed in the pressure and return lines at the engine. There shall be a water flow regulating valve installed for convenient operation by the driver. EXCEPTION: Type A Vehicles

8. All combustion-type heaters shall be approved by Underwriters Laboratories. (See Appendix).

IDENTIFICATION

1. Body shall bear words "SCHOOL BUS" in black letters at least 8 inches high on both front and rear of body or on signs attached thereto. Lettering shall be placed as high as possible without impairment of its visibility. Lettering shall conform to "Series B" of Standard Alphabets for highway signs.

2. Only signs and lettering approved by state law or regulation, limited to name of owner or operator and any number necessary for identification, shall appear on sides of bus.

INSIDE HEIGHT

Inside body height shall be nominal 72-inches or more, measured metal to metal, at any point on longitudinal center line from front vertical bow to rear vertical bow. EXCEPTION: Type A and B Vehicles

INSULATION

Ceiling and walls shall be insulated with proper material to deaden sound and to reduce vibration to a minimum. If thermal insulation is specified also, it shall be of fire-resistant material of type approved by Underwriters Laboratories, Inc. (See Appendix)

If floor insulation is required it may be 5-ply, at ⅝ -inches thick and/or it shall equal or exceed properties of exterior-type softwood plywood, C - D Grade as specified in standard issued by U.S. Department of Commerce. (See Appendix)

INTERIOR

1. Interior of bus shall be free of all unnecessary projections likely to cause injury. This standard requires inner lining on ceilings and walls. If ceiling is constructed so as to contain lapped joints, forward panel shall be lapped by rear panel and exposed edges shall be beaded, hemmed, flanged, or otherwise treated to minimize sharp edges.

2. Flammability of interior materials is covered by Federal Motor Vehicle Safety Standard No. 302.

LAMPS AND SIGNALS

1. Lamps on exterior of vehicle are covered by Federal Motor Vehicle Safety Standard 108.

2. Interior Lamps. Interior lamps shall be provided which adequately illuminate aisle and step-well.

3. School Bus Alternately Flashing Signal Lamps:

Definition: School bus red signal lamps are alternately flashing lamps mounted horizontally both front and rear, intended to identify a vehicle as a school bus and to inform other users of the highway that such vehicle is stopped on highway to take on or discharge school children.

School bus yellow signal lamps are alternately flashing lamps mounted horizontally both front and rear, intended to identify a vehicle as a school bus and to inform other users of the highway that such vehicle is about to stop on highway to take on or discharge school children.

a. Bus shall be equipped with two red lamps at rear of vehicle and two red lamps at front of vehicle.

b. In addition to four red lamps described in (a) above, four amber lamps shall be installed as follows: one amber lamp shall be located near each red signal lamp, at same level, but closer to vertical centerline of bus; system of red and amber signal lamps shall be wired so that amber lamps are energized manually, and red lamps are automatically energized (with amber lamps being automatically de-energized) when bus service door is opened.

c. Area around lens of each alternately flashing signal lamp and extending outward approximately 3 inches shall be painted black. In installations where there is no flat vertical portion of body immediately surrounding entire lens of lamp, a circular or square band of black approximately 3 inches wide, immediately below and to both sides of lens, shall be painted on body or roof area against which signal lamp is seen (from distance of 500 feet along axis of vehicle).

d. All flashers for alternately flashing red and amber signal lamps shall be enclosed in the body in a readily accessible location.

4. Turn signal and stop lamps.

a. Bus body shall be equipped with rear turn signal lamps which are at least seven(7) inches in diameter and meet specifications of the Society of Automotive Engineers. (See Appendix) These signals must be connected to the chassis hazard warning switch to cause simultaneous flashing of turn signal lamps when needed as vehicular traffic hazard warning. Turn signal lamps are to be placed as wide apart as practical and their centerline shall be approximately eight (8) inches below the rear windows. EXCEPTION: Type A Vehicle lamps must be 21 square inches in lens area.

b. Just inside the turn signal, there shall be installed at the same elevation, two seven (7) inch diameter stop lamps.

5. On all buses equipped with a monitor which monitors the front and rear lamps of the school bus, the monitor shall be mounted in full view of the driver. If the full circuit current passes through the monitor, each circuit shall be protected by a fuse or circuit breaker against any short circuit or intermittent shorts.

6. White Flashing Strobe Light: A white flashing strobe light, when installed, is intended to increase the visibility of the school bus on the highway during adverse visibility conditions. It shall have a single clear lens emitting light 360° around its vertical axis. It shall be located on the longitudinal centerline of the bus roof approximately ⅓ to ½ of the distance forward from the rear of the bus. It shall be controlled by a manual switch located in the instrument panel to the left of the driver. A pilot light shall indicate to the driver that the light is turned on.

7. Warning Device: Each school bus shall contain at least three (3)

reflectorized triangle road warning devices mounted in an accessible place in the driver's compartment. EXCEPTION: In Type A Vehicles the mounting location is optional.

METAL TREATMENT

All metal used in construction of bus body shall be zinc- or aluminum-coated or treated by equivalent process before bus is constructed. Included are such items as structural members, inside and outside panels, door panels, and floor sills; excluded are such items as door handles, grab handles, interior decorative parts, and other interior plated parts.

All metal parts that will be painted shall be (in addition to above requirements) chemically cleaned, etched, zinc-phosphate-coated, and zinc-chromate or epoxy primed or conditioned by equivalent process.

In providing for these requirements, particular attention shall be given lapped surfaces, welded connections of structural members, cut edges, punched or drilled hole areas in sheet metal, closed or box sections, unvented or undrained areas, and surfaces subjected to abrasion during vehicle operation.

As evidence that above requirements have been met, samples of materials and sections used in construction of bus body, when subjected to 1000-hour salt spray test as provided for in latest revision of ASTM designation; B-117 "Standard Method of Salt Spray (Fog) Testing" (See Appendix), shall not lose more than 10 percent of material by weight.

MIRRORS

Interior Mirror: Interior mirror shall be either clear view laminated glass or clear view glass bonded to a backing which retains the glass in the event of breakage. Mirror shall be a minimum of 6″ × 30″. Mirror shall have rounded corners and protected edges.

Exterior Mirrors: Each bus shall have a minimum of one exterior left side and one exterior right side rear view mirror with a minimum of 50 square inches each of flat mirror glass. EXCEPTION: Type A and B Vehicles shall be manufacturer's standard.

Each bus shall have a minimum of one exterior right side convex mirror with a minimum of 35 square inches to provide localized vision on the right side of the bus.

Cross-over Vision Mirror: When a rod 30 inches long is placed upright on the ground at any point along a traverse line 1 foot forward of the forward-most point of a school bus and extending the width of the bus: at least 7½ inches of the length of the rod shall be visible to the driver, either by direct view or by means of an indirect visibility system.

MOUNTING

Chassis frame shall support rear body cross member. Bus body shall be attached to chassis frame at each main floor sill, except where chassis components interfere, in such manner as to prevent shifting or separation of body from chassis under severe operation conditions.

OVERALL LENGTH

Overall length of bus shall not exceed 40 feet.

OVERALL WIDTH

Overall width of bus shall not exceed 96 inches excluding accessories.

RUB RAILS

1. There shall be one rub rail located on each side of bus approximately at seat level which shall extend from rear side of entrance door completely around bus body (except emergency door) to point of curvature near outside cowl on left side.

2. There shall be one rub rail located approximately at floor line which shall cover same longitudinal area as upper rub rail, except at wheelhousing, and shall extend only to radii of right and left rear corners.

3. Both rub rails shall be attached at each body post and all other upright structural members.

4. Both rub rails shall be 4 inches or more in width, shall be of 16-gauge steel or suitable material of equivalent strength, and shall be constructed in corrugated or ribbed fashion.

5. Both rub rails shall be applied outside body or outside body posts. Pressed-in or snap-on rub rails do not satisfy this requirement. EXCEPTION: For Type A and B Vehicles using chassis manufacturer's body, or Type C and D buses using rear luggage or rear engine compartment, rub rails need not extend around rear corners.

SANDERS

Where required or used, sanders shall:

1. Be of hopper cartridge-valve type.

2. Have metal hopper with all interior surfaces treated to prevent condensation of moisture.

3. Be of at least 100 pound (grit) capacity.

4. Have cover on filler opening of hopper, which screws into place, sealing unit airtight.

5. Have discharge tubes extending to front of each rear wheel under fender.

6. Have no-clogging discharge tubes with slush-proof, non-freezing rubber nozzles.

7. Be operated by electric switch with telltale pilot light mounted on instrument panel.

8. Be exclusively driver-controlled.

9. Have gauge to indicate hoppers need refilling when they are down to one-quarter full.

SEAT BELT FOR DRIVER

Seat belt for driver shall be provided. Belt shall be equipped with retractor on each side of sufficient quality and strength to keep it retracted and off floor when not in use.

SEATS AND CRASH BARRIERS

1. All seats shall have minimum depth of 15 inches.

2. In determining seating capacity of bus, allowable average rump width shall be:

   a. 13 inches where 3-3 seating plan is used.

   b. 15 inches where 3-2 seating plan is used.

3. Seat, seat back cushion and crash barrier shall be covered with a material having 42-ounce finished weight, 54 inches width, and finished vinyl coating of 1.06 broken twill, or other material with equal tensile strength, tear strength, seam strength, adhesion strength, resistance to abrasion, resistance to cold, and flex separation.

STEERING WHEEL

(See Chassis)

STEPS

1. First step at service door shall be not less than 12 inches and not more than 16 inches from ground, based on standard chassis specifications.

2. Service door entrance may be equipped with two-step or three-step step-well. Risers in each case shall be approximately equal. When plywood floor is used on steel, differential may be increased by thickness of plywood used.

   a. When three-step step-well is specified the first step at service door shall be approximately 10 to 14 inches from the ground when bus is empty, based on standard chassis specifications.

3. Steps shall be enclosed to prevent accumulation of ice and snow.

4. Steps shall not protrude beyond side body line.

5. Grab handle not less than 10 inches in length shall be provided in unobstructed location inside doorway. EXCEPTION: Type A and B Vehicles. Steps (if any) on Type A and B Vehicles not manufactured originally as school buses may be manufacturer's standard.

STEP TREADS

1. All steps, including floor line platform area, shall be covered with 3/16-inch rubber floor covering or other materials equal in wear resistance and abrasion resistance to top grade rubber.

2. Metal back of tread, minimum 24-gauge cold roll steel, shall be permanently bonded to ribbed rubber; grooved design shall be such that said grooves run at 90-degree angle to long dimension of step tread.

3. Three-sixteenth-inch ribbed step tread shall have a 1½-inch white nosing as integral piece without any joint.

4. Rubber portion of step treads shall have following characteristics:

   a. Special compounding for good abrasion resistance and high coefficient of friction.

   b. Flexibility so that it can be bent around a ½ -inch mandrel both at 130-degrees F and 20-degrees F without breaking, cracking, or crazing.

   c. Show a durometer hardness 85 to 95.

STIRRUP STEPS

There shall be at least one folding stirrup step or recessed foothold and suitably located handles on each side of the front of the body for easy accessibility for cleaning the windshield and lamps except when windshield and lamps are easily accessible from the ground. Standard does not apply to vehicles not originally manufactured as school buses. A step, in lieu of the stirrup steps, is permitted in or on the front bumper.

STOP SIGNAL ARM

Stop signal arm, if used, shall meet the applicable requirements of Society of Automotive Engineers J1133. (See Appendix) Flashing lamps in stop arm shall be connected to the alternately red flashing signal lamp circuits. Manual, vacuum, electric or air operation of stop signal arm is optional.

STORAGE COMPARTMENT

If tools, tire chains and/or tow chains are carried on the bus, a container of adequate strength and capacity may be provided. Such storage container may be located either inside or outside the passenger compartment but, if inside, it shall have a cover (seat cushion may not serve as this purpose) capable of being securely latched and be fastened to the floor convenient to either the service or emergency door.

SUN SHIELD

Interior adjustable transparent sun shield not less than 6″ × 30 ″ with a finished edge shall be installed in a position convenient for use by driver. EXCEPTION: Type A and B Vehicles.

TAILPIPE

Shall not extend beyond rear bumper.

UNDERCOATING

Entire underside of bus body, including floor sections, cross member, and below floor line side panels, shall be coated with rust-proofing compound for which compound manufacturer has issued notarized certification of compliance to bus body builder that compound meets or exceeds all performance requirements of Federal Specification TT-C-520a (See Appendix) using modified test procedures* for following requirements:

1. Salt spray resistance—pass test modified to 5% salt and 1,000 hours.
2. Abrasion resistance—pass.
3. Fire resistance—pass.

*Test panels are to be prepared in accordance with paragraph 4 6.12 of TT-C-520a with modified procedure requiring that tests be made on a 48-hour air cured film at thickness recommended by compound manufacturer.

Undercoating compound shall be applied with suitable airless or conventional spray equipment to recommended film thickness and shall show no evidence of voids in cured film.

VENTILATION

1. Body shall be equipped with suitable, controlled ventilating system of sufficient capacity to maintain proper quantity of air under operating conditions without opening of windows except in extremely warm weather.
2. Static-type non-closable exhaust ventilation shall be installed in low-pressure area of roof. EXCEPTION: Type A and B Vehicles.

WHEELHOUSING

1. The wheelhousing opening shall allow for easy tire removal and service.

2. Wheelhousing shall be attached to floor sheets in such a manner to prevent any dust, water, or fumes from entering the body. Wheelhousing shall be constructed of 16-gauge steel, or other material of equal strength.

3. The inside height of the wheelhousing above the floor line shall not exceed 12 inches.

4. The wheelhousing shall provide clearance for installation and use of tire chains on single and dual (if so equipped) power-driving wheels.

5. No part of a raised wheelhousing shall extend into the emergency door opening. EXCEPTION: Type A and B Vehicles.

WINDOWS

1. Each full side window shall provide unobstructed emergency opening at least 9 inches high and 22 inches wide, obtained by lowering window.

2. Push-out type, split-sash windows may be used.

WINDSHIELD WASHERS

A windshield washer system shall be provided.

WINDSHIELD WIPERS

1. A windshield wiping system, two-speed or more, shall be provided.

2. The wipers shall be operated by one or more air or electric motors of sufficient power to operate wipers. If one motor is used the wipers shall work in tandem to give full sweep of windshield.

WIRING

1. All wiring shall conform to current standards of Society of Automotive Engineers. (See Appendix)

2. Circuits:

   a. Wiring shall be arranged in circuits as required with each circuit protected by a fuse or circuit breaker. A system of color coding shall be used.

   b. Wiring shall be arranged in at least six regular circuits, as follows:

      (1) head, tail, stop (brake), and instrument panel lamps.

      (2) clearance and step-well lamps (step-well lamp shall be actuated when service door is opened).

(3) dome lamp.

(4) ignition and emergency door signal.

(5) turn signal lamps.

(6) alternately flashing signal lamps.

c. Any of above combination circuits may be subdivided into additional independent circuits.

d. Whenever heaters and defrosters are used, at least one additional circuit shall be installed.

e. Whenever possible, all other electrical functions (such as sanders and electric-type windshield wipers) shall be provided with independent and properly protected circuits.

f. Each body circuit shall be coded by number or letter on a diagram of circuits and shall be attached to the body in readily accessible location.

3. The entire electrical system of the body shall be designed for the same voltage as the chassis on which the body is mounted.

4. All wiring shall have an amperage capacity equal to or exceeding the designed load. All wiring splices to be done at an accessible location and noted as splices on wiring diagram.

5. A body wiring diagram of easy readable size shall be furnished with each bus body or affixed in an area convenient to the electrical accessory control panel.

6. Body power wire shall be attached to special terminal on the chassis.

7. All wires passing through metal openings shall be protected by a grommet.

8. Wires not enclosed within body shall be fastened securely at intervals of not more than 18 inches. All joints shall be soldered or joined by equally effective connectors.

SPECIAL EDUCATION VEHICLE STANDARDS

INTRODUCTION TO SPECIAL EDUCATION SCHOOL BUS OR MPV

The specifications in this section are intended to be supplementary to specifications in the chassis and body sections. In general, special education buses should meet all the requirements of those preceding sections plus those listed in this section. Since it is recognized by the entire industry that the field of transportation for special education passengers is characterized by special needs for individual cases and by a rapidly emerging technology for meeting these needs, a flexible, common-sense approach to the adoption and enforcement of specifications for these vehicles is prudent.

The Ninth National Conference recognized the rapidity of change in this area of transportation and addressed this fact by passing a resolution calling for special sessions at the 1981 NAPT/NASDPTS and NSTA Conferences to update the proceedings of the conference relating to minimum standards for special education school buses and auxiliary equipment.

By Federal Regulation, buses, including school buses, are defined as vehicles designed to carry ten or more passengers. Vehicles with less than ten passenger positions (including the driver) cannot be certified as buses. For this reason, the Federal vehicle classification Multipurpose Passenger Vehicle, or MPV, must be used by manufacturers in some cases for these vehicles in lieu of the classification School Bus. In determining passenger capacity, wheelchair positions are counted as passenger positions. This classification system while requiring compliance with a different set of Federal Standards for School Buses does not preclude the use of National School Bus Yellow paint or School Bus warning lamp systems.

GENERAL REQUIREMENTS

1. School buses designed for transporting children with special transportation needs shall comply with National Minimum Standards applicable to school buses. Because of the use of special equipment on these buses, certain modifications and/or exceptions in these standards shall be made, particularly in the bus body.

2. These standards address modifications as they pertain to school buses with a gross vehicle weight of ten thousand pounds or more and standard seating arrangement prior to modification that provides a capacity of ten or more children.

3. Any school bus that is used specifically for the transportation of children who are confined to a wheelchair and/or other mechanical restraining devices prohibiting their use of the regular service entrance, shall be equipped with a power lift.

4. Lift shall be located on the right side of the body, in no way attached to the exterior sides of the bus but confined within the perimeter of the school bus body when not extended.

SPECIAL SERVICE ENTRANCE

1. Bus bodies may have a special service entrance constructed in the body to accommodate a wheelchair lift for the loading and unloading of passengers.

2. The opening, to accommodate the special service entrance, shall be at any convenient point on the right (curb side) of the bus and far enough to the rear to prevent the door(s), when open, from obstructing the right front regular service door (excluding a regular front service door lift).

3. The opening may extend below the floor through the bottom of the body skirt. If such an opening is used, reinforcements shall be installed at the front and rear of the floor opening to support the floor and give the same strength as other floor openings.

4. The opening, with doors open, shall be of sufficient width to allow the passage of wheelchairs. The minimum clear opening shall be thirty (30) inches in width.

5. A drip moulding shall be installed above the opening to effectively divert water from entrance.

6. Entrance shall be of sufficient width and depth to accommodate various mechanical lifts and related accessories as well as the lifting platform.

7. Door posts and headers from entrance shall be reinforced sufficiently to provide support and strength equivalent to the areas of the side of the bus not used for service doors.

SPECIAL SERVICE ENTRANCE DOORS

1. A single door may be used if the width of the door opening does not exceed forty (40) inches.

2. Two doors shall be used if any single door opening would have to exceed forty (40) inches.

3. All doors shall open outwardly.

4. All doors shall have positive fastening devices to hold doors in the open position.

5. All doors shall be weather sealed and on buses with double doors, they shall be so constructed that a flange on the forward door overlaps the edge of the rear door when closed.

   If optional power doors are installed the design shall permit release of the doors for opening and closing by the attendant from the platform inside the bus.

6. When manually operated dual doors are provided the rear door shall have at least a one-point fastening device to the header.

   The forward mounted door shall have at least three-point fastening devices. One shall be to the header, one to the floor line of the body, and the other shall be into the rear door.

   These locking devices shall afford maximum safety when the doors are in the closed position.

   The door and hinge mechanism shall be of a strength that will provide for the same type of use as that of a standard entrance door.

7. Door materials, panels, and structural strength shall be equivalent to the conventional service and emergency doors. Color, rub rail extensions, lettering and other exterior features shall match adjacent sections of the body.

8. Each door shall have windows set in rubber compatible within one-inch of the lower line of adjacent sash.

9. Door(s) shall be equipped with a device that will actuate a green flashing visible signal located in the driver's compartment when door(s) is not securely closed and ignition is in "on" position.

10. A switch shall be installed so that the lifting mechanism will not operate when the lift platform door(s) is closed.

POWER LIFT

1. Lifting mechanism shall be able to lift minimum pay load of six hundred (600) pounds.

2. When the platform is in the fully up position, it shall be locked in position mechanically by means other than a support, or lug in the door.

3. Controls shall be provided that enable the operator to activate the lift mechanism from either inside or outside of the bus. There shall be a means of preventing the lift platform from falling while in operation due to a power failure.

4. Power lifts shall be so equipped that they may be manually raised in the event of power failure of the power lift mechanism.

5. Lift travel shall allow the lift platform to rest securely on the ground.

6. All edges of the platform shall be designed to restrain wheelchair and operator's feet from being entangled during the raising and lowering process.

7. Platform shall be fitted on both sides and rear with full width shields

(which extend above the floor line of the lift platform).

8. A restraining device shall be affixed to the outer edge (curb end) of the platform that will prohibit the wheelchair from rolling off the platform when the lift is in any position other than fully extended to ground level.

9. A self-adjusting, skid resistant plate shall be installed on the outer edge of the platform to minimize the incline from the lift platform to the ground level. This plate, if so designed, may also suffice as the restraining device described in item 8 above. The lift platform must be skid resistant.

10. A circuit breaker or fuse shall be installed between power source and lift motor if electrical power is used.

11. The lift mechanism shall be equipped with adjustable limit switches or by-pass valves to prevent excessive pressure from building in the hydraulic system when the platform reaches the full up position or full down position.

FASTENING DEVICES

1. Positive fastening devices shall be provided and attached to the floor or walls or both to insure that occupied wheelchairs or any other occupied types of ambulatory devices can be securely fastened in position.

RESTRAINING DEVICES

1. Seat frames may be equipped with attachments or devices to which belts, restraining harnesses, or other devices may be attached.

SPECIAL LIGHT

1. Lights shall be placed inside the bus to sufficiently illuminate lift area and shall be activated from door area.

AISLES

1. All aisles leading to the emergency door(s) from wheelchair area shall be of sufficient width (minimum thirty (30) inches) to permit passage of maximum size wheelchair.

SEATING ARRANGEMENTS

1. Flexibility in seat spacing to accommodate special devices shall be permitted due to the constant changing of passenger requirements.

GLAZING

1. Tinted glass may be installed in all doors, windows, and windshield. Tinted plastic may be installed in windows rear of the driver's compartment.

HEATERS

1. An additional heater(s) may be installed in the rear portion of the bus (behind wheel wells).

COMMUNICATIONS

1. All special education buses may be equipped with a two-way radio communication system.

REGULAR SERVICE ENTRANCE

1. In type "C" and "D" vehicles, there shall be three (3) step risers, of equal height, in the entrance well.

2. An additional fold-out step may be provided which will provide for the step level to be no more than six (6) inches from the ground level.

EXHAUST SYSTEM

1. The exhaust system shall be routed to the left of the right frame rail to allow for the installation of a lift mechanism that would travel through the floor on the right side of the vehicle.

TYPE A SCHOOL BUSES USED FOR SPECIAL TRANSPORTATION

1. This section pertains to vehicles of more than ten (10) persons capacity but less than ten thousand (10,000) pounds in GVW.

2. These vehicles shall meet the specifications of all the previous sections. EXCEPTION: In lieu of a power lift, a ramp device may be installed.

NATIONAL SCHOOL BUS YELLOW

The color known as National School Bus Yellow was designated as such by the 1939 National Conference on School Bus Standards. The National Bureau of Standards of the U. S. Department of Commerce assisted in developing this color and its colorimetric specifications, as follows:

C.I.E. Chromaticity coordinates		Daylight reflectance Y (%)			Dominant Wavelength (in millicrons)			Excitation Purity P (%)		
x	y	max.	std.	min.	max.	std.	min.	max.	std.	min.
.5211	.4549	–	41.	40.	584.5	583.5	582.5	–	93.7	89.0

At the 1980 Conference the colors in use were reviewed. A color standard was selected, slightly different from the above, and specific tolerances were chosen. These tolerances will insure a continuity of appearance from bus to bus, and within the same bus when different elements are finished or refinished at different times. Specification for the Standard Color, with light and dark tolerances (Upper and Lower Reflectances) are shown below in tabular form.

SPECIFICATION FOR STANDARD COLOR

For Source C			Reflectance Tolerances	
CIE Chromaticity Coordinates		Reflectance Y (%)	Upper	Lower
x	y			
.5089	.4408	40.14%	41.77%	38.45%

SCHOOL BUS OPERATIONS AND SAFETY APPENDICES

CONTENTS

SCHOOL BUS OPERATIONS AND SAFETY

APPENDICES

Appendix A

ACTIONS TO BE TAKEN DURING AND FOLLOWING OBSERVATION OF SCHOOL BUS ROUTES

When the transportation director rides the school bus for purposes of observation, here are some of the actions that should be taken during and following this observation:

1. Check driver's route and schedule for accuracy.

2. Determine that the driver stops only at authorized stops.

3. Check for operation of vehicle in accordance with prescribed regulations.

4. Observe the driver-pupil relationship.

5. Check the conditions at the school for a satisfactory area to unload and load the students and evidence of supervision.

6. Note hazardous road conditions.

7. Note the nature, frequency, and locations of violations of the school bus stop law.

8. Observe condition of bus, e.g., cleanliness, tires, windows, emergency exit(s), first aid kits, fire extinguishers, seats, etc.

9. Note driver attitude toward other motorists and pedestrians. Following completion of observation, a report should be written, discussed with driver (and others, as appropriate), then filed with the driver's permanent record.

Appendix B

SCHOOL BUS DRIVER APPLICATION

(Example of a form that may be used)

Name____

Present Address__________________ Phone No. ______________

How long have you lived at present address?________________

Last previous address_______________________________

How long did you live there?_____ Social Security No. __________

Do you have any physical impairments that could interfere with the duties of a school bus operator?____________________________

Current driver's license: Operator's ____________

Chauffeur's ____________ Other ____________

Number ____________ State ____________

Have you had any type of vehicle accident in the last three years?

Yes ______ No ______. __________________________

If yes, give dates and explain

Have you been convicted for a moving traffic violation in the last three years?

Yes ______ No ______. __________________________

If yes, give dates and explain

Has your driver's license been suspended or revoked during the last three years?

Yes ______ No ______.

To the best of my knowledge, the answers to the above are full and correct.

Date ____________ Signature________________________

REFERENCES

Do not use relatives. Include at least one businessman and one professional person.

	NAME	ADDRESS	TEL.	OCCUPATION
1.				
2.				
3.				
4.				
5.				

Appendix C

SCHOOL BUS DRIVER PHYSICAL EXAMINATION FORM

(Example of a form that may be used)

Name __________________ Address____________________________

Have you ever had: 1. Heart trouble? ______ 2. Epilepsy? ______
3. Fainting spells? ______ 4. Diabetes? ______
5. Tuberculosis? ______
If "yes" to any of the above, explain:______________________________

____

Signature of driver____
Visual acuity* (if individual wears glasses, test and record acuity with and without glasses.)
Without glasses: R 20/______ L 20/______ B 20/______
With glasses: R 20/______ L 20/______ B 20/______
Field of vision ____________ degrees Depth perception____________
Color perception ____________ Muscular anomalies____________
Hearing without hearing aid: Right ____________
Left ____________
Heart sounds: At apex murmur ____________ At base murmur______
Rhythm ________________ Enlargement indicated____________
Pulse: Rate ________________ Regularity________________
Blood pressure: Systolic ____________ Diastolic________________
Condition of arteries: Sclerosis ____________ Pulsations__________
Lungs: Rales ______ Breath sounds ______ Chest X-ray__________
Weight ____________ Height____________________________
Extremities: Deformities____________________________________
Routine Office urinalysis____________________________________
Evidence of infectious disease, mental disability, emotional instability, or drug addiction____

____

Remarks regarding any condition not within normal limits____________

____

After examination I find______________________________________
is /   / is not /   / free from any ailment, disease, or defect that might affect his or her ability to safely operate a school bus.
Date ____________ ____________________________________

Licensed Physician

---

*Visual examination may be performed by either a licensed physician or a licensed optometrist.

Appendix D

INSTRUCTIONS FOR CONDUCTING EMERGENCY EXIT DRILLS

Due to the increased number of pupils being transported and the ever-increasing number of accidents on the highways there is a need to instruct pupils on how to properly vacate a school bus in case of an emergency. In an emergency it is possible for pupils to jam the emergency door by all trying to get out of the door at the same time. In order to help avoid a situation of this type, schools should organize and conduct emergency exit drills for all pupils who may ride the school buses.

There are several different drills:

1. Everyone exits through the front entrance door.
2. Everyone exits through the rear emergency door.
3. Front half exits through the front door and rear half exits through the rear door. (see diagram)

There is possible danger when a pupil jumps from the rear emergency door exit.

Reasons for actual emergency evacuations:

1. Fire or danger of fire. The bus should be stopped and evacuated immediately if the engine or any portion of the bus is on fire. Pupils should move to a safe place 100 feet or more from the bus and remain until the driver of the bus has determined that no danger exists. Being near an existing fire and unable to move the bus away, or near the presence of gasoline or other combustible material should be considered as "danger of fire," and pupils should be evacuated.
2. Unsafe position. In the event that a bus is stopped due to accident, mechanical failure, road conditions, or human failure the driver must determine immediately whether it is safer for pupils to remain in the bus or to evacuate.
3. The driver must evacuate if:
    a. The final stopping point is in the path of any train or adjacent to any railroad tracks.
    b. The stopping position of the bus may change and increase the danger. If, for example, a bus should come to rest near a body of water or precipice where it could still move and go into the water or over a cliff, it should be evacuated. The driver should be certain that the evacuation is carried out in a manner which affords maximum safety for the pupils.
    c. The stopping of the bus is such that there is danger of collision.

In normal traffic conditions, the bus should be visible for a distance of 300 feet or more. A position over a hill or around a curve where such visibility does not exist should be considered reason for evacuation.

Important factors pertaining to school bus evacuation drills:

1. Safety of pupils is of the utmost importance and must be considered first.

2. All drills should be supervised by the principal or by persons assigned to act in a supervisory capacity.

3. The bus driver is responsible for the safety of the pupils; however, in an emergency the driver might be incapacitated and would not be able to direct the pupil emergency evacuation. School patrol members, appointed pupils, or adult monitors should direct these drills. It is important to have regular substitutes available.

   Pupil qualifications:

   a. Maturity.

   b. Good citizenship.

   c. Live near end of bus line.

   Pupil should know how to:

   a. Turn off ignition switch.

   b. Set emergency brake.

   c. Summon help when and where needed.

   d. Use fire axe or kick out windows.

   e. Set flags and flares.

   f. Open and close doors, account for all pupils passing his station.

   g. Help small pupils off bus.

   h. Perform other assignments.

66 PASSENGER BUS

(3 pupils to a seat)

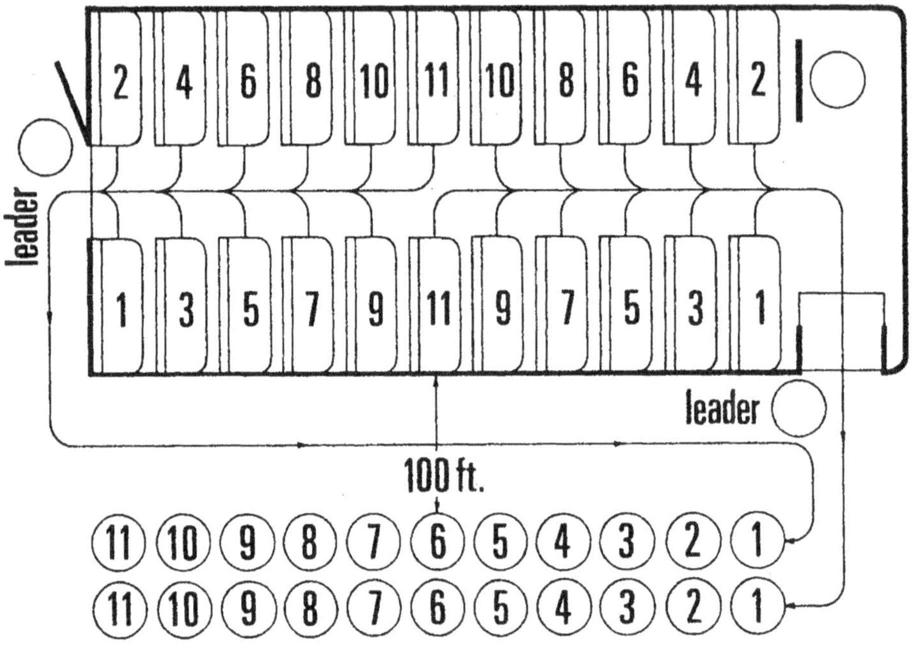

66 passenger bus—11 rows of seats on each side
60 passenger bus—10 rows of seats on each side
54 passenger bus—9 rows of seats on each side
48 passenger bus—8 rows of seats on each side

4. Written consent from parent should be obtained before assigning a pupil as a leader.

5. School bus evacuation drills should be organized in a manner similar to fire drills held regularly in schools. The drills should be held more often during fall and spring months, preferably when bus arrives at the school building with the pupils.

6. Drills should be held on school property and not on bus route.

7. Types of bus drills held should be varied.

8. Drivers should stay in bus during evacuation drills. Be sure that the parking brake is set, ignition off, and transmission in gear.

9. Do not permit pupils to take lunch boxes, books, etc., with them when they leave the bus—getting the pupil off safely in the shortest time possible and in an orderly fashion is the objective.

10. The pupils should go to a distance of at least 100 feet from the bus in an "emergency drill" and remain there in a group until given further directions by the leader.

11. All pupils should be given an opportunity to participate, including those pupils who only ride a bus on special trips.

12. Each pupil should be instructed in the proper safety precautions while riding the bus and in drill procedures.

13. Instruct pupils in how and where to get help. Instructions and telephone numbers should be posted or otherwise carried in the school buses.

Appendix E

PLANNING SCHOOL SITES FOR SCHOOL BUS SAFETY

1. In the selection of school sites, major consideration should be given to the safety of pupils riding school buses. School buses will be forced to utilize the roads in and around the school site plus public highways leading into the school area. High density traffic flow near school exits and entrances due to the proximity of freeways, periodic commercial traffic, or massive commuter traffic from industrial plants should be avoided. It must be recognized in many cases that the area designated for the school site has been selected prior to the hiring of an architect. It is suggested, therefore, that this information be issued to boards of education and municipal planning authorities alerting them to the dangers inherent in the process of site selection. It is also suggested that boards of education discuss the selection with the superintendent of schools, traffic engineers, and the state office of School Plant Planning and solicit their help in evaluating possible school sites.

2. The location of the school plant on a site should be determined so as to provide safe means of entrance and egress for all pupils. When boards of education are considering school sites, the state, county, and local roads servicing the area should have a minimum 30 foot paved width where loading and unloading is contemplated off the main thoroughfare. If it is necessary to load or unload pupils on the main thoroughfare in front of the school, at least a 40-foot-wide paved road should be provided.

3. It is possible that boards of education may have land donated to them that could be classified as unsafe for busing due to its traffic density, type of terrain, or lack of safe loading and unloading facilities. The cost of eliminating these unsafe conditions may exceed the purchase price of a more desirable parcel of property. In such instances it might be wiser not to accept the donated land but attempt to secure a site that would provide for the safety of students that would have to be transported to the school.

4. All school bus traffic should be considered as one-way traffic flow, preferably with the service door side of the bus always next to the loading and unloading zone.

5. Wherever possible, separation should be maintained between bus traffic and regular flow as constituted by parent, pupil, service, teacher, and administrative traffic.

6. Whenever possible, roads should not be constructed that completely encircle a school. Areas that pupils must cross to engage in outside activities should be free of all vehicular traffic.

7. All school bus roads entering into or exiting from main arteries should have a 50- to 100-foot radius turn on inner edge of pavement. Within the school site, roads should have at least a 60-foot radius on

inner edge of pavement on all curves. At least a 50-foot tangent section should be provided between reverse curves. In order to minimize driveway entrance and exit widths, island construction may be required. Driveway openings must conform to local requirements, and in particular, driveway openings on state highways should be approved by the state highway department.

8. It is recommended that curbing, with suitable drainage, be constructed on all roads utilized by the school bus within the school site. A minimum of 30 feet should be maintained for one-way traffic and 36 feet for two-way traffic. Roads should be wider on all curves.

9. It is desirable to separate all parking from the loading zone utilized by the school bus.

10. In the construction of parking areas, it might be advantageous if only the visitor parking area were located in close proximity to the school. Care should be exercised in the placement of these areas to preclude the visitor from crossing the school bus traffic pattern.

11. Architects, prior to the designing and laying-out of roads and parking lots, should consult with the school administration on the following items:

    A. Total number of pupils and school personnel.

    B. Number of present and projected pupils to be transported.

    C. Number of buses.

    D. Type of schedule.

        a. Staggered.

        b. Single (one opening and closing time).

    E. Extra-curricular activities that would necessitate use of school buses.

12. Where buses are parked on the school grounds consideration should be given to the reflective surfaces of windows, doors, and windshields in order to prevent undue glare from these parked vehicles being transmitted to the pupils in the classroom.

13. Attention should be given in planning school bus parking and loading areas so as to encourage diagonal parking. Positioning of buses in slant formation provides the safest method of loading and leaving school grounds. Where this is not possible, bumper-to-bumper positioning of buses would be the next best solution. Either type of parking should exclude the necessity for backing the school bus.

14. In the construction of sidewalks for pupils walking to school,

consideration should be given to the elimination of crosswalks in front of buses.

15. In the analysis of many architects' plans for school buildings, bus canopies were included for consideration. In the majority of cases such units were not considered feasible for schools with large enrollments. Canopies are advantageous in schools where handicapped pupils are in attendance. Height of the canopy, obviously, should accommodate the highest school buses.

16. In the construction of curbs, where school buses will be utilized, consideration should be given to the performance specifications set forth by the state highway department.

17. In areas that will be constantly utilized by heavy-weight school buses, the type of pavement and base should be that specified by the state highway department.

18. All roads within the school site should be graded to avoid dips and hollows that would impair the vision of motorists using the roadways. It is suggested that a maximum standard of not more than a 5 per cent grade be allowed for roads on school sites. At entrance and exit points a maximum grade of 2 per cent should be adhered to.

19. Blind corners or intersections should be eliminated.

20. In the planning of a school and the location of access and service roads, conditions should never be set up that would require school buses to be backed on the school premises.

21. All pupil loading and unloading should be provided for on the school site.

22. Wherever possible, parents should be assigned a separate pupil pickup point some distance from the school bus loading areas. Accident-inducing conditions are created by parents picking up and discharging pupils haphazardly in the area in front of and adjacent to the building. The condition is greatly increased during inclement weather.

23. In the provision of loading facilities, consideration should be given to separate areas especially designed for handicapped pupils, including entrance ramps and handrails.

24. In the planning of all roads and loading areas, architects should take into consideration the fact that emergency vehicles must have access to the school at all times.

25. Care should be taken in the planting of trees and shrubbery on the school site so as not to obstruct the vision of the motorist.

26. Where necessary, traffic control devices should be provided to assist school traffic in entering the regular traffic flow.

Appendix F

EVALUATION CHECKLIST FOR SCHOOL BUS DRIVEWAYS IN THE VICINITY OF THE SCHOOL

NAME OF THE SCHOOL:________________ DATE: ____________
LOCATION OF THE SCHOOL:______________________________

		YES	NO	DOES NOT APPLY
1.	School bus loading and unloading areas are provided on the school site.	____	____	________
2.	When loading and unloading of school pupils take place on main thoroughfare in front of the school, the roadway has a minimum width of 40 feet of hard surface.	____	____	________
3.	The driveway leading to and from the loading and unloading area for school buses has a minimum width of 30 feet of paved surface.	____	____	________
4.	If diagonal parking is provided for buses in the loading and unloading area, a minimum width of 60 feet of paved surface is available.	____	____	________
5.	Parking for loading and unloading of pupils at school is bumper-to-bumper ( ) or diagonal ( ): in either case, the necessity for backing does not exist.	____	____	________
6.	The school bus is not required to back anywhere on school property.	____	____	________
7.	All school bus movement on the school grounds is one-way in a counter-clockwise direction.	____	____	________
8.	School bus traffic does not completely encircle the school building.	____	____	________
9.	The driver has proper sight distance at all points along the driveway.	____	____	________
10.	Crosswalks for pupils do not exist within the entrance to the school bus driveway.	____	____	________

11. Separation is maintained between school bus traffic and all other traffic. ____ ____ ________

12. Vehicular pickup points for non-bus pupils are on separate driveway from that used by school buses. ____ ____ ________

13. Curbing and suitable drainage are provided along driveways. ____ ____ ________

14. Curbing and driveway construction comply with state highway specifications. ____ ____ ________

15. At ingress and egress areas to the school there is a minimum radius on inner edge of driveway pavement of from 50 to 100 feet. ____ ____ ________

16. On the school site there is a minimum radius of inner edge of driveway pavement of 60 feet. ____ ____ ________

17. Between reverse curves, at least a 50-foot tangent section is provided. ____ ____ ________

18. At ingress and egress points a maximum grade of 2 per cent is adhered to. ____ ____ ________

19. A maximum grade of 5 per cent is adhered to on the school bus driveway within the school site. ____ ____ ________

NOTE: A "yes" answer for each of the items indicates a well-planned traffic pattern for school buses.

SIGNATURES:
Person making the report: ________________________
Director of School Transportation: ________________________

APPENDIX G

RECOMMENDED PROCEDURES FOR SCHOOL BUS DRIVERS AT RAILROAD GRADE CROSSINGS

A. General

1. The driver of any school bus, with or without pupils shall come to a complete stop no closer than fifteen feet, and within fifty feet from the rails nearest the front of the bus.

2. Drivers making stops for railroad crossings shall observe traffic. Bus speed shall be reduced far enough in advance of the stop to avoid trapping other motorists in panic stops or rear-end collisions with the bus. On multiple lane roadways, all stops must be made in the far right lane whenever possible.

3. Turn signal lights shall be operated in their hazard mode when permitted by state statute or regulation. No other signs or signals will be activated from the bus while stopped or stopping for the railroad crossing.

4. When the bus is stopped, the driver shall fully open the service door, listen and look in both directions along the track or tracks for approaching engines, trains, or train cars.

5. For improved vision and hearing, a window at the driver's left should be opened and all noisy equipment (fans, etc.) should be turned off until the bus has cleared the crossing.

6. If the view of the track or tracks is obstructed for one thousand feet in either direction, no portion of the bus may be driven onto the tracks until the driver has made certain that no train is approaching. Although railroad signals may indicate the tracks are clear, the driver must develop and use visual and audible senses to determine whether or not it is safe to proceed.

7. The school bus driver shall always drive across the tracks in an appropriate low gear and will not change gears while crossing the tracks.

8. After a train has passed the crossing, the bus driver shall not drive the bus onto any tracks until the driver is certain that no train, hidden by the first train, is approaching on an adjacent track. Familiarity with train time schedules has no place in school bus operation.

B. At Crossings Controlled by Signals

1. The driver of a school bus which has stopped at any railroad track or tracks at which there is in operation any flashing red lights and/or bell shall not proceed across such track or tracks

unless by authorization from a law enforcement officer or flagman.

2. At crossings controlled by traffic signals (usually on freeways), the bus driver shall obey the traffic signals.

C. At Crossings Controlled by Crossing Gate or Barrier

1. No bus driver shall drive the bus through, around or under any crossing gate or barrier at a railroad crossing while such gate or barrier is closed or being opened or closed.

2. The bus driver must never accept a lack of movement as an indication that the device is working or out of order. A driver must always consider a railroad grade crossing as conclusive warning of danger and shall not cross the tracks until the driver has determined that no train is approaching.

D. Weather Conditions

During wet, stormy, or foggy weather, before placing part of the bus on the tracks, the driver must know that the crossing can be made in safety. Any use of flares or warning signals must be taken as an additional warning of danger.

E. Behavior of Pupils

When any school bus must stop for any railroad track at grade, all pupils must be silent until crossing is completed. Such signal for silence shall be given by the school bus driver.

Appendix H

Measuring Fleet Performance

How do you best measure the safety performance of a school bus fleet? The total number of accidents from month to month and from year to year may be an adequate yardstick for school records but accident totals can be misleading if there have been changes in the number of buses or the length of routes. You cannot use accident totals to compare the safety performance of one school district with that of another.

A common denominator is needed that will mean the same thing from month to month, year to year, and school to school. The accident frequency rate, the number of accidents per 1,000,000 vehicle miles, is one such common denominator. The formula for computing an accident frequency rate is as follows:

$$\text{Accident Rate} = \frac{\text{Accidents} \times 1{,}000{,}000}{\text{Vehicle Miles}}$$

Example: There are five buses in a fleet. They travel a total of 4,000 miles per month. During one month one accident takes place. The frequency rate would be as follows:

$$\frac{1 \times 1{,}000{,}000}{4{,}000} = 250$$

A rate of 250 is very high indeed, considering that inter-city buses achieve an average yearly rate of 11.3. But one month is too short a period of exposure to present a fair picture of a fleet's safety performance. An average rate for nine months or a year is usually considered standard.

In the above example, if the school bus fleet operated for nine months with only one reportable accident, the rate would be:

$$\frac{1 \times 1{,}000{,}000}{36{,}000} = 27.77$$

www.ingramcontent.com/pod-product-compliance
Lightning Source LLC
Chambersburg PA
CBHW081808300426
44116CB00014B/2278
9781799301134